PENGUIN BOOKS — GREAT IDEAS

Of Human Freedom

Epictetus

c. AD 55–135

Epictetus

Of Human Freedom

TRANSLATED BY ROBERT DOBBIN

PENGUIN BOOKS — GREAT IDEAS

PENGUIN BOOKS

Published by the Penguin Group
Penguin Books Ltd, 80 Strand, London WC2R ORL, England
Penguin Group (USA) Inc., 375 Hudson Street, New York, New York 10014, USA
Penguin Group (Canada), 90 Eglinton Avenue East, Suite 700, Toronto, Ontario, Canada M4P 2Y3
(a division of Pearson Penguin Canada Inc.)
Penguin Ireland, 25 St Stephen's Green, Dublin 2, Ireland (a division of Penguin Books Ltd)
Penguin Group (Australia), 250 Camberwell Road, Camberwell, Victoria 3124, Australia
(a division of Pearson Australia Group Pty Ltd)
Penguin Books India Pvt Ltd, 11 Community Centre, Panchsheel Park, New Delhi – 110 017, India
Penguin Group (NZ), 67 Apollo Drive, Rosedale, North Shore 0632, New Zealand
(a division of Pearson New Zealand Ltd)
Penguin Books (South Africa) (Pty) Ltd, 24 Sturdee Avenue, Rosebank, Johannesburg 2196,
South Africa

Penguin Books Ltd, Registered Offices: 80 Strand, London WC2R ORL, England

www.penguin.com

This translation taken from *Discourses and Selected Writings* first published by Penguin
Classics 2008
This selection first published in Penguin Books 2010

014

Translation copyright © Robert Dobbin, 2008
Selection copyright © Robert Dobbin, 2010

The discourses are taken from: Book I 1, 2, 12, 24 and 25; Book II 1, 13, 15, 17 and 18;
Book III 1 and 20; Book IV 1, 2 and 4

All rights reserved

Set in 11/13 Dante MT Std
Typeset by TexTech International
Printed and bound in Great Britain by Clays Ltd, Elcograf S.p.A.

ISBN: 978-0-141-19235-2

www.greenpenguin.co.uk

MIX
Paper | Supporting
responsible forestry
FSC
www.fsc.org   FSC® C018179

Penguin Books is committed to a sustainable
future for our business, our readers and our planet.
This book is made from Forest Stewardship
Council™ certified paper.

Contents

Contents

I
Concerning what is in our power and what is not

[1] In general, you will find no art or faculty that can analyse itself, therefore none that can approve or disapprove
of itself. [2] The art of grammar is restricted to analysing
and commenting on literature. Music is confined to the
analysis of harmony. [3] Consequently neither of them
analyses itself. Now, if you are writing to a friend, the art
of grammar will help you decide what words to use; but
it will not tell you whether it is a good idea to write to your
friend in the first place. Music is no different; whether this is
a good time to sing and play, or a bad one, the art of music
by itself cannot decide.

[4] So what can? The faculty that analyses itself as well
as the others, namely, the faculty of reason. Reason is
unique among the faculties assigned to us in being able to
evaluate itself – what it is, what it is capable of, how valuable it is – in addition to passing judgement on others.

[5] What decides whether a sum of money is good?
The money is not going to tell you; it must be the faculty
that makes use of such impressions – reason. [6] Reason,
in addition, takes the measure of music, grammar and
the other arts, judging their benefit and deciding when
it's best to use them.

[7] So it's only appropriate that the gods have given us

the best and most efficacious gift: the ability to make good use of impressions. Other capacities they did not put in our power. [8] Was it because they did not want to? Personally, I believe that they would have endowed us with those others too, had they been able. But they were not. [9] Since we are on earth, you see, bound to a material body and material things, we can hardly avoid being limited by these extraneous factors.

[10] Well, what does Zeus say? 'Epictetus, if it were possible, I would have made your little body and possessions both free and unrestricted. [11] As it is, though, make no mistake: this body does not belong to you, it is only cunningly constructed clay. [12] And since I could not make the body yours, I have given you a portion of myself instead, the power of positive and negative impulse, of desire and aversion – the power, in other words, of making good use of impressions. If you take care of it and identify with it, you will never be blocked or frustrated; you won't have to complain, and never will need to blame or flatter anyone. [13] Is that enough to satisfy you?'

'It's more than enough. Thank you.'

[14] And yet, while there is only the one thing we can care for and devote ourselves to, we choose instead to care about and attach ourselves to a score of others: to our bodies, to our property, to our family, friends and slaves. [15] And, being attached to many things, we are weighed down and dragged along with them. [16] If the weather keeps us from travelling, we sit down, fret, and keep asking, 'Which way is the wind blowing?' 'From the north.' 'That's no good. When will it blow from the west?' 'When it wants to, or rather when Aeolus wants it

to; because God put Aeolus in charge of the winds, not you.' [17] What should we do then? Make the best use of what is in our power, and treat the rest in accordance with its nature. And what is its nature? However God decides.

[18] 'Must I be beheaded now, and alone?' Well, do you want everyone to be beheaded just because misery loves company? [19] Why not hold out your neck the way Lateranus did at Rome, when condemned by Nero to be beheaded? He held out his neck willingly to take the blow – but the blow was deficient, so he recoiled a bit, but then had enough self-command to offer his neck a second time. [20] And prior to that, when Epaphroditus, Nero's freedman, approached a certain man and asked him about the grounds of his offence, he replied, 'If I want anything, I will tell it to your master.'

[21] What should we have ready at hand in a situation like this? The knowledge of what is mine and what is not mine, what I can and cannot do. [22] I must die. But must I die bawling? I must be put in chains – but moaning and groaning too? I must be exiled; but is there anything to keep me from going with a smile, calm and self-composed?

'Tell us your secrets.'

[23] 'I refuse, as this is up to me.'

'I will put you in chains.'

'What's that you say, friend? It's only my leg you will chain, not even God can conquer my will.'

[24] 'I will throw you into prison.'

'Correction – it is my body you will throw there.'

'I will behead you.'

3

'Well, when did I ever claim that mine was the only neck that couldn't be severed?'

[25] That's the kind of attitude you need to cultivate if you would be a philosopher, the sort of sentiments you should write down every day and put in practice.

[26] Thrasea used to say, 'I would sooner be killed today than banished tomorrow.' [27] And what did Musonius say to him? 'If you choose death because it is the greater evil, what sense is there in that? Or if you choose it as the lesser evil, remember who gave you the choice. Why not try coming to terms with what you have been given?'

[28] Agrippinus used to say, 'I don't add to my troubles.' To illustrate, someone once said to him, 'You are being tried in the Senate – [29] good luck.' But it was eleven in the morning, and at that hour he was in the habit of taking his bath and exercise. 'Let us be off to exercise.' [30] When he was done, word came that he had been condemned. 'To exile,' he asked, 'or death?' 'Exile.' 'And my estate, what about that?' 'It has not been confiscated.' 'Well then, let us go to my villa in Aricia and have lunch there.' [31] This shows what is possible when we practise what is necessary, and make our desire and aversion safe against any setback or adversity. [32] 'I have to die. If it is now, well then I die now; if later, then now I will take my lunch, since the hour for lunch has arrived – and dying I will tend to later.' How? As someone who knows that you have to return what belongs to somebody else.

2

How a person can preserve their proper character in any situation

[1] Man, the rational animal, can put up with anything except what seems to him irrational; whatever is rational is tolerable. [2] Physical hardships are not intolerable by nature. The Spartans, for instance, gladly submit to being whipped because they are taught that it is done for good reason. [3] But what about being hanged – isn't that intolerable? Well, people frequently go and hang themselves, whenever they judge that it is a reasonable course of action.

[4] In short, reflection will show that people are put off by nothing so much as what they think is unreasonable, and attracted to nothing more than what to them seems reasonable.

[5] But standards of reasonableness and unreasonableness vary from one person to the next – just as we consider different things good or bad, harmful or beneficial. [6] Which is why education has no goal more important than bringing our preconception of what is reasonable and unreasonable in alignment with nature.

[7] But this not only involves weighing the value of externals, it also means considering what agrees with our own, individual nature. [8] For one person it is reasonable to be a bathroom attendant, because he only

thinks about what punishment and privation lie in wait for him otherwise, and knows that if he accepts the assignment he will be spared that pain and hardship. [9] Someone else not only finds such a job intolerable for him personally, but finds it intolerable that anyone should have to perform it. [10] But ask me, 'Shall I be a bathroom attendant or not?' and I will tell you that earning a living is better than starving to death; so that if you measure your interests by these criteria, go ahead and do it. [11] 'But it would be beneath my dignity.' Well, that is an additional factor that you bring to the question, not me. You are the one who knows yourself – which is to say, you know how much you are worth in your own estimation, and therefore at what price you will sell yourself; because people sell themselves at different rates.

[12] So, for instance, Agrippinus told Florus to 'Go ahead' when he was debating whether to attend Nero's festival, maybe even participate. [13] But when Florus asked him why he was not going himself, Agrippinus answered, 'I don't even consider the possibility.' [14] Taking account of the value of externals, you see, comes at some cost to the value of one's own character.

[15] So if you want to know if life or death is better, the answer I give is, 'Life.' [16] If you ask about pain versus pleasure, I say, 'Pleasure is preferable.'

'But if I refuse to participate in Nero's festival, he will kill me.'

[17] Go ahead and participate, then – but I still refuse.

'Why?'

Because you think of yourself as no more than a single thread in the robe, whose duty it is to conform to the mass of people – just as a single white thread seemingly has no wish to clash with the remainder of the garment. [18] But I aspire to be the purple stripe, that is, the garment's brilliant hem. However small a part it may be, it can still manage to make the garment as a whole attractive. Don't tell me, then, 'Be like the rest,' because in that case I cannot be the purple stripe.

[19] In his actions Helvidius Priscus showed his awareness of this principle. When Emperor Vespasian sent him word barring him from the Senate, his response was, 'You can disqualify me as a senator. But as long as I do remain a member I must join the assembly.' [20] 'Well join, then, but don't say anything.' 'Don't call on me for my vote and I won't say anything.' 'But I must call on you for your vote.' 'And I have to give whatever answer I think is right.' [21] 'Answer, and I will kill you.' 'Did I ever say I was immortal? You do your part, and I will do mine. It is your part to kill me, mine to die without flinching; your part to exile me, mine to leave without protest.'

[22] And what did Priscus accomplish, who was but a single man? Well, what good does the purple stripe do the robe? Its lustre is a good example to the rest. [23] If it had been someone else in the same situation whom the emperor barred from entering the Senate, he would have probably said, 'I'm so grateful you can spare me.' [24] In fact, the emperor would not have even bothered to bar him, well aware that the man would either sit there like a blockhead or, if he did speak, would only mouth words he knew that Caesar wanted to hear – and would pile additional inanities on besides.

[25] A certain athlete, at risk of dying unless his genitals

were amputated, made a comparable choice. His brother, a philosopher, went and asked him, 'Well, my brother, what's it going to be? Will you have them amputated, and return to life in the gymnasium?' The man refused to submit to the indignity, however, and summoned the will to die. [26] Someone asked, 'Did he choose death as an athlete or as a philosopher?' 'As a man,' Epictetus said, 'one who had competed at the level of the Olympic Games, where he was a familiar figure, and a victor more than once – no occasional visitor to the local gym. [27] Someone else might have even allowed his head to be removed, if his life could have been saved thereby.' [28] That's what I mean by having consideration for one's character. And it shows how weighty a factor it can be when it is allowed a regular role in one's deliberations.

[29] 'Come, Epictetus, shave off your beard.'

If I am a philosopher, I will not shave it off.

'But I will cut off your head.'

If that will do you any good, then cut it off.

[30] Someone asked, 'But how do we know what is in keeping with our character?'

Well, how does the bull realize its own strength, rushing out to protect the whole herd when a lion attacks? The possession of a particular talent is instinctively sensed by its owner; [31] so if any of you are so blessed you will be the first to know it. [32] It is true, however, that no bull reaches maturity in an instant, nor do men become heroes overnight. We must endure a winter training, and can't be dashing into situations for which we aren't yet prepared.

[33] Consider at what price you sell your integrity;

but please, for God's sake, don't sell it cheap. The grand gesture, the ultimate sacrifice – that, perhaps, belongs to others, to people of Socrates' class. [34] 'But if we are endowed by nature with the potential for greatness, why do only some of us achieve it?' Well, do all horses become stallions? Are all dogs greyhounds? [35] Even if I lack the talent, I will not abandon the effort on that account. [36] Epictetus will not be better than Socrates. But if I am no worse, I am satisfied. [37] I mean, I will never be Milo either; nevertheless, I don't neglect my body. Nor will I be another Croesus – and still, I don't neglect my property. In short, we do not abandon any discipline for despair of ever being the best in it.

3
On satisfaction

[1] On the subject of the gods, there are those who deny the existence of divinity outright. Others say that God exists, but is idle and indifferent and does not pay attention to anything. [2] A third group says that God exists and is attentive, but only to the workings of the heavens, never affairs on earth. A fourth group says that he does attend to earthly affairs, including the welfare of humanity, but only in a general way, without worrying about individuals. [3] And then there is a fifth group, Odysseus and Socrates among them, who say that 'I cannot make a move without God's notice.'

[4] Before doing anything else we need to examine these views separately to decide which are true and which are false. [5] Because if the gods do not exist, what sense can be made of the command to 'follow the gods'? And how can it be a sensible goal if they exist, but do not have any cares? [6] Even supposing that they exist and care, if that care does not extend to people, and, in point of fact, to me personally, it is still no worthwhile goal.

[7] The intelligent person, after due consideration of the question, will decide to submit his will to the ruler of the universe, as good citizens submit to the laws of the state.

[8] Education should be approached with this goal in mind: 'How can I personally follow the gods always, and

how can I adapt to God's government, and so be free?' [9] Freedom, you see, is having events go in accordance with our will, never contrary to it.

[10] Well – is freedom the same as madness? Of course not. Madness and freedom are poles apart. [11] 'But I want my wishes realized, never mind the reason behind them.' [12] Now, that's madness, that's insanity. Freedom is something good and valuable; to wish arbitrarily for things to happen that arbitrarily seem to you best is not good, it's disgraceful.

How do we approach the practice of writing? [13] Do I want to write the name 'Dion' whatever way I please? No, I learn to want to write it the way it is supposed to be written. The case is the same with music, [14] the same with every art and science; it would not be worth the trouble to learn them, otherwise, if they accommodated everyone's wishes. [15] And freedom, the greatest possession of all, is the last thing you would expect to be different, where wishes are given carte blanche. Getting an education means learning to bring our will in line with the way things happen – which is to say, as the ruler of the universe arranged. [16] He arranged for there to be summer and winter, abundance and lack, virtue and vice – all such opposites meant for the harmony of the whole; and he gave us each a body and bodily parts, material belongings, family and friends.

[17] It is with this arrangement in mind that we should approach instruction, not to alter the facts – since this is neither allowed, nor is it better that it should be – but in order to learn the nature of what concerns us, and keep our will in line with events. [18] Can we avoid people?

How is that possible? And if we associate with them, can we change them? Who gives us that power? [19] What is the alternative – what means can be found for dealing with them? One that ensures that we remain true to our nature, however other people see fit to behave. [20] That's not what you do, though. No, you gripe and protest against circumstance. If you're alone, you call it desolation, if you're in company you describe them all as swindlers and backstabbers; you curse your own parents, your children, your siblings and neighbours. [21] When you are by yourself you should call it peace and liberty, and consider yourself the gods' equal. When you're with a large group you shouldn't say you're in a mob or crowd, but a guest at a feast or festival – and in that spirit learn to enjoy it.

What is the downside for those who refuse to accept it? To be just as they are. [22] Is someone unhappy being alone? Leave him to his isolation. Is someone unhappy with his parents? Let him be a bad son, and grumble. Is someone unhappy with his children? Let him be a bad father. [23] 'Throw him in jail.' What jail? The one he is in already, since he is there against his will; and if he is there against his will then he is imprisoned. Conversely, Socrates was *not* in prison because he chose to be there.

[24] 'But my leg is crippled.'

Slave, are you going to be at odds with the world because of one lame leg? Shouldn't you rather make the world a gift of it, and gladly return it to the one who gave it to you originally? [25] Are you going to make Zeus your enemy, and set your face against the Fates, with whom Zeus spun the thread of your destiny at the moment you were born, laying out his plans for you?

[26] You ought to realize, you take up very little space in the world as a whole – your body, that is; in reason, however, you yield to no one, not even to the gods, because reason is not measured in size but sense. [27] So why not care for that side of you, where you and the gods are equals?

[28] 'It's my bad luck to have awful parents.'

Well, you couldn't very well choose them beforehand, saying, 'Let this man have intercourse with this woman, at this particular, so that I can be conceived.' [29] Your parents had to come first, then you had to be born the way you are, of parents the way *they* are.

[30] Does that mean you have to be miserable? Let's suppose you didn't understand what you had the power of vision for; it would be your bad luck if you decided to close your eyes just at the moment a beautiful painting passed before you. You are even unluckier for being oblivious to the fact that you have the power of patience to deal with your difficulties. [31] You forget the virtues of character you have in reserve, just when problems that they can control present themselves, and you could use their help.

[32] You should thank the gods for making you strong enough to survive what you cannot control, and only responsible for what you can. [33] The gods have released you from accountability for your parents, your siblings, your body, your possessions – for death and for life itself. [34] They made you responsible only for what is in your power – the proper use of impressions. [35] So why take on the burden of matters which you cannot answer for? You are only making unnecessary problems for yourself.

4
How we should struggle with circumstance

[1] The true man is revealed in difficult times. So when trouble comes, think of yourself as a wrestler whom God, like a trainer, has paired with a tough young buck. [2] For what purpose? To turn you into Olympic-class material. But this is going to take some sweat to accomplish. From my perspective, no one's difficulties ever gave him a better test than yours, if you are prepared to make use of them the way a wrestler makes use of an opponent in peak condition.

[3] Now we are sending you to Rome as a spy. And we don't want one who is easily frightened, or one who will turn back at the first sound of noise, or glimpse of shadow, announcing hysterically that the enemy is practically at the gates. [4] If you tell us on your return, 'Conditions are terrible in Rome, everywhere death, exile, poverty, informants – everything a shambles. Fly, the enemy is upon us!' [5] – we will respond by telling you in future to keep your forecasts to yourself. Our only mistake was in sending a spy like you in the first place.

[6] Diogenes went scouting before you did and came back with a very different report. Death, he said, was not evil because it was not dishonourable. Reputation was the empty noise of fools. [7] And he said other things that

helped remove the element of fear from pain and poverty. In his manner of life he preferred the minimum of clothing to a purple gown, and the bare ground to a bed, however soft. [8] And as proof of such claims, he produced his assurance, his serenity, his freedom – as well as his tough, radiant physique.

[9] 'There is no enemy nearby,' he said. 'All is peace and tranquillity.'

'Explain, Diogenes.'

'Look for yourself: am I wounded, disabled or in flight from any enemy force?'

[10] That's the kind of spy we honour. *You* bring us back a report full of a lot of random noise. Go off and make a better search, this time without the trepidation.

[11] 'What should I do then?'

What do you do when you leave a ship? Do you walk off with the rudder and oars? No; you leave with your own gear, your oil-flask and wallet. So just remember what belongs to you, and you won't lay claim to what doesn't.

[12] The emperor says to you, 'Remove your broad hem.'

'Very well, I'll wear the narrow hem.'

'Remove that too.'

'All right, I'll wear the ordinary toga now.'

'Take your toga off.'

'Fine, I'll go naked.'

[13] 'Now your very composure provokes me.'

'Take my whole body, then.'

Is there any reason to fear someone to whom I stand ready to surrender my miserable corpse?

[14] But so-and-so will not leave his estate to me. Well? I forgot that none of it was mine. How then do we call it mine? As we call the bed in an inn mine. If the innkeeper dies and leaves you his bed, fine; but if he leaves it to someone else, then *he* will have it, and you will find a replacement. [15] And if you don't, then you will have to sleep on the ground. Only rest easy there and snore away, because, remember, tragedies take place among the rich – among kings, and potentates. No poor man swells a tragedy except as a member of the chorus. [16] Kings start off well enough: 'Deck the palace halls.' But then around the third or fourth act, we get, 'O Cithaeron, why did you receive me?' [17] Fool, where are your crowns, your diadem? Even your guards can't help you now.

[18] So when you stand before one of those tyrants, just bear in mind that you are in the presence of a tragic figure – and not the actor, either, but Oedipus himself.

[19] 'But he's so lucky to be able to walk around with an entourage.'

Well, I too mingle with the masses and so am attended by an entourage. [20] The chief thing to remember is that the door is open. Don't be a greater coward than children, who are ready to announce, 'I won't play any more.' Say, 'I won't play any more,' when you grow weary of the game, and be done with it. But if you stay, don't carp.

5
More on the same theme

[1] If what we've been saying is true and we aren't being ridiculous, or merely pretending to believe that what is good or bad for us lies in the will and that we are indifferent to everything else – then why do we continue to experience fear and anxiety? [2] No one has power over our principles, and what other people do control we don't care about. So what is your problem, still?

[3] 'My problem is that I want specific instructions on how to act in line with these principles.'

What other orders do you need than those Zeus has given you already? He has given you what is your own unrestricted and unrestrained; what is not yours he has made restricted and restrained. [4] What commandment, then, did you arrive with when he sent you here? 'Protect what belongs to you at all costs; don't desire what belongs to another.' Trustworthiness is your own, decency and a sense of shame; no one can take them from you or prevent you from using these qualities except yourself – which you do the moment you begin to care about what isn't yours, surrendering what *is* yours in the process.

[5] With such directions and commands from Zeus, what additional ones do you hope to get from me? Am I greater or more to be trusted? [6] Keep his commandments and you won't need others. And as proof that he has delivered them to you, bring your preconceptions to

bear. Bring the arguments of philosophers. Bring what you've often heard, and often said yourself; what you've read, and what you've practised.

[7] Just how long should we apply these precepts that we have from God, before breaking up the game? [8] Just so long as the game remains a pleasure. At the Saturnalia a king of the revels is chosen by chance, because this is the convention. Then our 'king' hands out orders: 'Drink up! You there, mix the wine! You, sir, give us a song! You, join the party; while you there – get lost!' And we play along with him, so that the game will not be spoiled on our account. [9] But if the 'king' says, 'Imagine that you are unhappy,' and I demur, who is going to force me? [10] If, on the other hand, the programme calls for the re-enactment of Achilles' quarrel with Agamemnon, and the actor in the role of king says to me, 'Go and get Briseis away from Achilles,' [11] I'll go. When he says, 'Return,' I'll return.

The way we handle hypothetical arguments can also serve as a model for our behaviour. 'Let's assume that it is night.'

'Fine.'

'Then is it day?'

'No, because I've accepted the hypothesis that it is night.'

[12] 'Let's assume, in the manner of a game or play, that you pretend to believe that it is night.'

'OK.'

'Now, believe that it really *is* night.'

[13] 'That does not follow from the hypothesis.'

The same rules apply in life: 'Let's assume you've come upon hard times.'

'Granted.'

'Then you are unfortunate.'

'Yes.'

'And suffering.'

'Yes.'

'Now believe that what has happened to you is bad.'

'That does not follow from the hypothesis. Besides, there is another who won't let me.'

[14] How long should we submit to the rules of the game? As long as it serves my turn, and I find the part congenial. [15] Some dour, inflexible types will say, 'I can't eat at this man's table if it means listening to his war stories again: "I told you, friend, how I scrambled up the hill; now we came under renewed bombardment . . ."' [16] But another person in the same situation might say, 'The meal is what matters; let him rattle on to his heart's content.' [17] It is for you to arrange your priorities; but whatever you decide to do, don't do it resentfully, as if you were being imposed on. And don't believe your situation is genuinely bad – no one can make you do that. [18] Is there smoke in the house? If it's not suffocating, I will stay indoors; if it proves too much, I'll leave. Always remember – the door is open.

[19] 'Do not remain in Nicopolis,' they say to me; so I don't remain there.

'Don't stay in Athens either.'

So I quit Athens.

'Not Rome either.'

So I abandon Rome.

[20] 'Live on Gyara.'

But for me living on Gyara amounts to more smoke in

my house than I can stand. So I depart to the one place no one can stop me from going to, where everyone is made welcome. [21] And when I remove my last piece of clothing – my skin – then no one can lay a hold of me any longer. [22] Which is why Demetrius was emboldened to say to Nero, 'You threaten me with death, but nature threatens *you*.'

[23] If I cherish my body, I make a slave of myself, if I cherish my property, I make a slave of myself; [24] because I've disclosed the means to make me captive. When a snake pulls back its head, right away I think, 'Hit it just there, on the part that it's protecting.' In the same way you may be sure that whatever you are seen to protect, that will become your enemy's focus of attack. [25] Keep this in mind, then there will be no one you will need to fear or flatter.

[26] 'But I want to sit in the senators' gallery.'

Look, the crowd is of your own creation, you're treading on your own toes.

[27] 'But how else am I to get a clear view of the stage?'

If you don't want to be crowded, don't attend the theatre. What's the difficulty? Or wait until the show is over, then seat and sun yourself at leisure in the senators' seats. [28] In general, remember that it is we who torment, we who make difficulties for ourselves – that is, our opinions do. What, for instance, does it mean to be insulted? [29] Stand by a rock and insult it, and what have you accomplished? If someone responds to insult like a rock, what has the abuser gained with his invective? If, however, he has his victim's weakness to exploit, then his efforts are worth his while.

[30] 'Strip him.' What do you mean, 'him'? Take his garment, you mean, and remove that. 'I have insulted you.' 'A lot of good may it do you.' [31] That is what Socrates practised, maintaining always the same even temper. But it seems that we would practise and study anything rather than how to remain free and unenslaved.

[32] 'Philosophers speak in paradoxes.'

And what of the other arts – are they different? What is more paradoxical than cutting into a person's eye to restore his vision? If someone suggested this procedure to a person ignorant of medicine, they would laugh in the practitioner's face. [33] Little wonder, then, if many of the truths of philosophy also impress the masses as paradoxical.

6
That confidence does not conflict with caution

[1] To some people, perhaps, what we philosophers say will appear impossible. But let us investigate, all the same, whether it's true that in our daily lives we can act with both caution and confidence. [2] It seems impossible because the two are evidently opposites – and opposites (supposedly) cannot coexist. But what most people consider strange I think can be explained on the following hypothesis: [3] if we are talking about using confidence and caution on the same objects, we might fairly be accused of trying to reconcile irreconcilables. But our claim does not involve anything so strange.

[4] We have often said, and shown, that the use of impressions represents for us the essence of good and evil, and that good and evil have to do with the will alone. And if that is true, [5] then nothing is impractical in the philosophers' advice to 'Be confident in everything outside the will, and cautious in everything under the will's control.' [6] For if evil is a matter of the will, then caution is needed there; and if everything beyond the will and not in our control is immaterial to us, then those things can be approached with confidence. [7] And so, you see, that's how we can be cautious and confident at the same time – and, in fact, confident owing to our caution. For,

being on our guard against evils, we approach things whose nature is *not* evil in a spirit of assurance.

[8] Instead, however, we act like deer. When deer are frightened by the feathers, they seek safety in the hunters' nets. Confusing ruin with refuge, they come to an ill-timed death. [9] Similarly, fear afflicts us in matters outside the will's control, while we act confidently and casually in matters dependent on the will as if they were of no importance. [10] To be deceived or rash, to act shamelessly or with unbridled lust – none of this matters to us as long as we have success in affairs outside the will. Death, exile, pain and ill repute – there you will find the impulse to tremble and run away.

[11] So, you would expect when error involves the things of greatest importance, our natural confidence is perverted into rashness, thoughtlessness, recklessness and shamelessness. At the same time, all fear and agitation, we exchange our natural caution and reserve for meekness and timidity. [12] Transfer caution to the will and the functions of the will, and the mere wish will bring with it the power of avoidance. But if we direct it at what is outside us and is none of our responsibility, wanting instead to avoid what's in the control of others, we are necessarily going to meet with fear, upset and confusion. [13] Death and pain are not frightening, it's the fear of pain and death we need to fear. Which is why we praise the poet who wrote, 'Death is not fearful, but dying like a coward is.'

[14] So be confident about death, and caution yourself against the fear of it – just the opposite, in other words, of what we are doing now. Now we shrink from death,

whereas our views about death hardly concern us, we hardly give them a thought, and are completely apathetic. [15] Socrates used to call such fears 'hobgoblins', and rightly so; just as masks scare and frighten children since they haven't seen them before, we react to events in much the same way and for much the same reason.

[16] What is a child? Ignorance and inexperience. But with respect to what it knows, a child is every bit our equal. [17] What is death? A scary mask. Take it off – see, it doesn't bite. Eventually, body and soul will have to separate, just as they existed separately before we were born. So why be upset if it happens now? If it isn't now, it's later. [18] And why now, if that happens to be the case? To accommodate the world's cycle; because the world needs things to come into being now, things to come into being later – and it needs things whose time is now complete.

[19] Pain too is just a scary mask: look under it and you will see. The body sometimes suffers, but relief is never far behind. And if that isn't good enough for you, the door stands open; otherwise put up with it. [20] The door needs to stay open whatever the circumstances, with the result that our problems disappear. [21] The fruit of these doctrines is the best and most beautiful, as it ought to be for individuals who are truly educated: freedom from trouble, freedom from fear – freedom in general. [22] The masses are wrong to say that only freeborn men are entitled to an education; believe the philosophers instead, who say that only educated people are entitled to be called free. [23] I will explain. What else is freedom but the power to live our life the way we want?

'Nothing.'

Do you want to live life doing wrong?

'No.'

Therefore, no one doing wrong is free. [24] Do you want to live your life in fear, grief and anxiety?

'Of course not.'

So no one in a state of constant fear is free either. By the same token, whoever has gained relief from grief, fear and anxiety has gained freedom. [25] What confidence, then, can we have in our own dear legislators when they say that only freeborn people are entitled to an education, when the philosophers contend that only people already educated can be considered free? God will not allow it, you see.

[26] 'What about a master who performs the ceremony of manumitting a slave? Is nothing accomplished by that?'

Certainly it is – the master has performed the ceremony; and, on top of that, he has paid a five per cent tax to the state.

[27] 'But his slave – hasn't he come by his freedom in the process?'

No more than he has instantly come by peace of mind. I mean, consider your own case: you have slaves, and the power to free them. [28] But what master, I wonder, do you yourself serve? Money? Women? Boys? The emperor or one of his subordinates? It has to be one of them, or you wouldn't fret about such things.

[29] This is why I so often repeat to you the need to think about them and have these thoughts ready to hand, namely, the knowledge of what you should treat with confidence, and what you should treat with caution –

that you can treat with confidence whatever lies outside the will, but must treat with caution what lies within.

[30] But you say, 'Didn't I read to you, and didn't you take note of my performance?'

[31] I noticed your clever phrases, yes – and you can have them. Show me instead how you practise desire and aversion to get what you want and avoid what you do not want. As for those treatises of yours, if you have any sense, you will go and burn them.

[32] 'But wasn't Socrates a writer, and a prolific one at that?' Yes, but for what purpose? Since there wasn't always someone available whose ideas he could examine or who could examine Socrates' own in turn, sometimes he would test and examine himself, forever subjecting to scrutiny one assumption or another. [33] That's the writing of a real philosopher; whereas pretty phrases in dialogue form he leaves to others – aesthetes and idlers who lie about and have no patience with logical reasoning because they're too stupid.

[34] Even now, if the opportunity presents itself, I know you will go off to read and make public those compositions, and you'll pride yourself on being fluent in the dialogue form. [35] Don't do it, man. What I would rather hear from you is, 'Look how I don't fail in my desires, or have experiences I don't want. I'll prove it to you in the case of death, I'll prove it to you in the case of physical pain, in the case of prison, of condemnation, and ill repute.' That's the real test of a youth fit to finish school. [36] Forget about that other stuff, don't let people hear you giving public recitations; and even if someone praises you, restrain yourself, be content to look like a nobody or know-nothing.

[37] Show them this, though, that you know how not to fail in your desires or experience what you don't desire. [38] Let others practise lawsuits, solve logical puzzles or syllogisms. Your duty is to prepare for death and imprisonment, torture and exile – [39] and all such evils – with confidence, because you have faith in the one who has called on you to face them, having judged you worthy of the role. When you take on the role, you will show the superiority of reason and the mind over forces unconnected with the will. [40] Then that paradox will no longer seem so paradoxical or absurd – that we should be confident and cautious at the same time: confident in relation to things outside the will, cautious about things within.

7
On nerves

[1] Whenever I see a person suffering from nervousness, I think, well, what can he expect? If he had not set his sights on things outside man's control, his nervousness would end at once. [2] Take a lyre player: he's relaxed when he performs alone, but put him in front of an audience, and it's a different story, no matter how beautiful his voice or how well he plays the instrument. Why? Because he not only wants to perform well, he wants to be well received – and the latter lies outside his control.

[3] He is confident as far as his knowledge of music is concerned – the views of the public carry no weight with him there. His anxiety stems from lack of knowledge and lack of practice in other areas. Which are what? [4] He doesn't know what an audience is, or what approval from an audience amounts to. Although he knows well enough how to play every note on the lyre, from the lowest to the highest, the approval of the public – what it means and what real significance it has – this he does not know and has made no effort to learn. [5] Necessarily, then, he is going to get nervous and grow pale. Now, I won't go so far as to say that he's not a true musician if I see that he suffers from stage fright. But I can say one thing – several things, in fact.

[6] I can start by calling him a stranger and say, 'This person has no idea where he's living, and for all his time

in residence here still doesn't know the laws of the country or its customs. He does not know what is permitted and what is not. Furthermore, he has never taken the trouble to call on a lawyer who will tell him, and explain how things operate here. [7] He won't sign a contract without knowing how to draft one properly, or hiring somebody who does. He isn't casual about signing for loans or offering guarantees. But when it comes to desire, aversion, impulse, plans and projects, he applies himself to all of these without benefit of legal counsel. [8] How do I know? He wants what he cannot have, and does not want what he can't refuse – and isn't even aware of it. He doesn't know the difference between his own possessions and others''. Because, if he did, he would never be thwarted or disappointed.

Or nervous.

Just think: [9] we aren't filled with fear except by things that are bad; and not by them, either, as long as it is in our power to avoid them. [10] So, if externals are neither good nor bad, while everything within the sphere of choice is in our power and cannot be taken away by anyone, or imposed on us without our compliance – then what's left to be nervous about? [11] We agonize over our body, our money, or what the emperor is going to decree – never about anything inside us.

I mean, do we worry whether we are going to make an error in judgement? No, because it is under our control. Or having an unnatural urge? No again. [12] So if you see someone pale with nerves, be like a doctor who diagnoses liver trouble based on a patient's yellow skin. Say, 'This man's desire and aversion are unhealthy, they aren't functioning properly, they're infected. [13] Because nothing else can account for his change in colour, his shivering, his chattering teeth, and "this constant fretting and shifting from foot to foot".'

[14] All of which explains why Zeno was not nervous about his meeting with Antigonus. What Zeno valued Antigonus had no power over, and as a philosopher he cared nothing for the things that the king did command. [15] It was Antigonus who was anxious before their meeting. Naturally – he wanted to make a good impression, which was beyond his control. Zeno, for his part, had no wish to please the king; no expert needs validation from an amateur. [16] So what do I need *your* approval for? You don't know the measure of a man, you haven't studied to learn what a good or a bad person is, and how each one gets that way. No wonder you're not a good person yourself.

[17] 'How do you make that out?'

It is not in a good person's nature to grieve, complain or whine; they don't go pale, tremble and say, 'What kind of hearing or reception will he give me?' [18] Idiot, that's his concern – don't concern yourself with other people's business. It's his problem if he receives you badly.

'True.'

And you cannot suffer for another person's fault. So don't worry about the behaviour of others.

[19] 'All right, but I worry about how I will talk to him.'

Can't you talk to him any way you like?

'I'm afraid that I may say something gauche.'

[20] Look, when you are about to spell the name 'Dion', are you afraid that you will slip up?

'No.'

And why not? It's because you have practice in writing the name.

'True.'

And you would have the same confidence reading it.

'Yes.'

The reason is that any discipline brings with it a measure of strength and confidence in the corresponding arts. [21] Now, you have practice speaking. What else did they teach you at school?

'Syllogisms and changing arguments.'

But why, if not to be accomplished in conversation? And by accomplished I mean refined, assured, intelligent, not easily flustered or refuted – and fearless, on top of all that.

'Agreed.'

[22] Well, then, you are in the position of a soldier on horseback who is about to face a mere foot soldier, on ground that you have gone over and he has not. And still you're nervous?

'But he can literally kill me!'

[23] Well, then, speak the truth, you sorry specimen, don't put on airs and call yourself a philosopher. Face up to who your betters are. As long as you have this attachment to the body, be ready to submit to anyone or anything of superior physical force.

[24] As for speaking, Socrates must have practised the art, look at his answer to the Thirty Tyrants, his defence before the jury, his conversations in jail. Diogenes too had practised how to speak, witness the free and easy way he talked to Alexander, Philip, the pirates and the

person to whom the pirates sold him as a slave. [26] As for you, go back to your work and don't ever leave it. Settle back in your alcove, think up new syllogisms, and share them with your friends. [27] You are plainly not cut out for the role of public leader.

8

To people who cling hard to certain of their decisions

[1] Some people suppose that the virtue of resolution, when considered in connection with the fact that nature made the will free and untrammelled, and everything else blocked, checked, slavish and external, entails that our decisions should all be honoured to the extent of never backing off from one an inch. [2] No – the decision first must be well founded. I mean, I like a body to be strong, but strong with the energy that comes of good health and training, not the kind that comes of some manic disorder. [3] If you are taking pride in having the energy of a lunatic, I have to say, 'Friend, you need a therapist. This is not strength, but a kind of infirmity.'

[4] In a different sense, this ailment affects the minds of people who misconstrue our philosophy. A friend of mine, for instance, arbitrarily decided that he was going to starve himself to death. [5] When I heard that he was already three days into his fast, I went and asked him to explain.

'I made my decision,' he said.

[6] 'Yes, but what drove you to it? Look, if it is the right decision, we are ready to sit by your side and help you make the passage. But if it was a reckless decision, it should be open to change.'

[7] 'But we must stick with a decision.'

'For heaven's sake, man, that rule only applies to sound decisions. I suppose next you will decide that it is night now, and refuse to change your mind because you don't want to. You will repeat, "We must stick with a decision." [8] Begin with a firm foundation; evaluate your decision to see if it is valid – then there will be a basis for this rigid resolve of yours. [9] If your foundation is rotten or crumbling, not a thing should be built on it, and the bigger and grander you make it, the sooner it will collapse.

[10] 'With no good reason, you are taking the life of an old friend of mine, one who shares both cities with me, the big one and the small. [11] And while busy killing and doing away with an innocent man, you keep saying, "We must stick with a decision." [12] If the idea of killing me should ever occur to you, would the same principle apply, I wonder?'

[13] Well, with great difficulty the man was finally prevailed on to relent. But there are some people today whom there is just no persuading. I have come to understand that saying which I did not fully appreciate until now: 'A fool cannot be convinced or even compelled to renounce his folly.' [14] God save me from fools with a little philosophy – no one is more difficult to reach.

'I've made a decision.'

Yes, so have lunatics. But the more fixed their delusions, the more medication they require. [15] Do what sick people do, call on the doctor and say to him, 'Doctor, I'm sick and need your help. I promise to follow whatever you prescribe.' [16] Similarly, I expect to hear from you, 'I am lost and don't know what I should do. I've come to you to find out.' Instead, I get, 'Talk to me about anything else; in this matter my mind's made up.' [17] What else am I supposed to talk to you about? Nothing is more important than that I cure you of the conviction that 'We must stick with a decision, and never back down' is too crude a law. This is deranged, not healthy, resolution.

[18] 'I want to die, even though I don't have to.'

Why? What has happened?

'I made that decision.'

[19] Good thing it wasn't me you decided needed to go.

'I don't take money for my services.'

Why not?

'That was my decision.'

Realize that this irrationality means one day you might well switch to accepting money, and with the same degree of passion announce, 'This is my decision.' [20] You're like someone afflicted with certain illnesses, which manifest in different parts of the body at different times. It's the same with the unhealthy mind; what view it will incline to no one can ever guess. And when this arbitrariness is reinforced by strength of purpose, the illness becomes past help or healing.

9

How to adapt preconceptions to everyday instances

[1] The first thing a pretender to philosophy must do is get rid of their presuppositions; a person is not going to undertake to learn anything that they think they already know. [2] We come to the study of philosophy rattling off what should and should not be done, what's good, what's bad, and what's disgraceful. On this basis, we are quite prepared to pass out praise, blame, censure, or condemnation, subtly distinguishing good habits from bad.

[3] So what do we need philosophers for, if we know it all already? We want to learn what we don't presume to know – namely, problems of logic. We want to learn what those philosophers teach because it is supposed to be keen and clever. [5] Well, it is ridiculous to imagine that you will learn anything but what you want to learn; in other words, you can't hope to make progress in areas where you have made no application.

Many people, however, make the same mistake as the orator Theopompus. He criticized Plato for wanting to define every little thing. [6] 'Did no one before you,' he says, 'use the words "good" and "just"? Or if we did, were we ignorant of what each of them meant – were we making empty sounds bereft of sense?' [7] Look, Theopompus, no one denies that we had an inborn idea and preconception of these terms. What we lacked was the ability to apply them correctly. We had not yet organized them with a view to determining the class of things each of them belongs to.

[8] You might as well put the same challenge to doctors: 'Didn't we use the words "sick" and "healthy" before Hippocrates came along, or were we talking nonsense?' [9] Well, we had a concept of what 'healthy' means, yes, but even now we can't agree on how to adapt it. There's one doctor who says, 'Withhold his food,' while another says, 'Make him eat.' One says, 'Bleed her,' another says, 'She needs a transfusion.' And the cause of this chaos is none other than our still-unrealized ability to apply the concept of 'healthy' to particular cases.

[10] The same problem occurs in the conduct of life. 'Good', 'bad', 'useful', 'harmful' – these words are part of everyone's vocabulary, we all have a preconception of what they signify. But is it developed and complete? [11] Prove it – apply it correctly to particular things. Now Plato, for his part, associates definitions with his preconception of what is 'useful'; you, however, categorize them as useless. [12] Both of you cannot be right. Some people associate the idea of the good with wealth, or pleasure, or health; others plainly do not. [13] Because if all of us who use these words are not just blowing smoke, and we don't need help clarifying their preconceptions, why is there any misunderstanding, conflict or blame on either side?

[14] But why refer to conflict between different people, and bring up that? Just take yourself – if you are good at applying your preconceptions, why are you internally

conflicted and confused? [15] We will ignore for now the second field of study, to do with impulse and the art of applying impulse to appropriate acts. Let's skip the third field too, concerning assent – [16] I'll give you a pass on both. Let's stay with the first; it furnishes almost tangible proof that you are not good at applying preconceptions. [17] If your present desires are realistic – realistic for you personally – why are you frustrated and unhappy? If you are not trying to escape the inevitable, then why do you continue to meet with accident and misfortune? Why do you get what you do not want, and don't get what you do? [18] This is categorical proof of inner confusion and unhappiness. I want something to happen, and it fails to happen, or I don't want something to happen, and it does – and can any creature be more miserable than I?

[19] It is just this that Medea could not tolerate, and which drove her to slay her children – a magnificent act from one point of view, it shows she had the right idea of what it means to have one's desires dashed. [20] 'I'll have my revenge on the man who hurt and humiliated me. But what good are the usual types of punishment? How should it happen then? I will kill my children. But I will punish myself in the process . . . [21] Well – what of it?'

Behold the ruin of a noble soul. She did not know, in effect, that obtaining our desire is not done by looking outside ourselves for help, or by changing or rearranging circumstance. [22] Don't want your husband, and nothing that you want will fail to come. Don't want to stay with him at any price, don't wish to stay in Corinth – in short, don't want anything except what God wants, and no one will stop or stay you, any more than they can stand in the way of God. [23] When you have him as your leader, and conform your will and desire to his, what fear of failure can you have?

[24] Attach your desire to wealth and your aversion to poverty: you won't get the former, but you could well end up with the latter. You will fare no better putting your faith in health, status, exile – any external you care to name. [25] Hand your will over to Zeus and the gods, let them administer it; in their keeping, your happiness is assured.

[26] But please stop representing yourself as a philosopher, you affected fool! You still experience envy, pity, jealousy and fear, and hardly a day passes that you don't whine to the gods about your life. [27] Some philosopher! You learned syllogisms and changing arguments. Good, now try unlearning them, if you can, and make a fresh start. Wake up to the fact that so far you have barely touched the subject. [28] Begin to fashion your future in such a way that nothing happens contrary to your desire and nothing that you desire fails to materialize.

[29] Give me one student with *that* ambition when he presents himself at school, one committed to *that* kind of training, one who says, 'To me those other things are worthless; it's enough if one day I can live without sorrow and frustration, if I can lift up my head like a free person in the face of circumstance and look to heaven as a friend of God, without fear of anything that might happen.' [30] Show me such a person, so I can say, 'Come, child, take what you deserve. You were born to honour philosophy with your patronage – these halls, these

books, these lectures, they all belong to you.' [31] Then, after he's tackled and mastered this field of study, I will wait until he returns and says, 'I want to be free from fear and emotion, but at the same time I want to be a concerned citizen and philosopher, and attentive to my other duties, towards God, my parents, my siblings, my country, and my guests.' [32] Welcome to the second field of study, this is yours as well. [33] 'But I've already mastered the second field of study; I want to be faultless and unshakeable, not just when I'm awake, but even when I'm sleeping, even when I'm drunk or delirious.' You are a god, my child, you are headed for the stars.

[34] But no, what I get instead is, 'I want to read Chrysippus' treatise on the Liar.' Is that your plan? Then go and jump in the lake and take your ridiculous plan with you. What good could come of it? Your unhappiness will persist the whole time you are reading it, and your anxiety will not abate a bit during a reading of the thing before an audience.

[35] Here's how you behave: 'Shall I read to you, brother, then you to me?'

'Man, it's marvellous the way you write.'

'Well, it's uncanny how you capture Xenophon's style.'

[36] 'And *you* have caught Plato's manner.'

'And you Antisthenes'!'

Then, having indulged each other in your fatuous fancies, you go back to your former habits: your desires and aversions are as they were, your impulses, designs and plans remain unchanged, you pray and care for the same old things. [37] And so far from looking for someone to bring you to your senses, you are distinctly offended by any advice or correction. You say, 'He's nothing but a mean old man; when I left him he showed no sign of sorrow. He didn't say, "My, it's a dangerous journey you're going on, child. I'll light a candle if you come through safely." [38] That's what he would say if the man had any compassion.' And what a blessing it would be for a person like you to come through safely, calling for many candles to be lit! Really, you deserve to be immortal and impervious to misfortune.

[39] As I said, then, this presumption that you possess knowledge of any use has to be dropped before you approach philosophy – just as if we were enrolling in a school of music or mathematics. [40] Otherwise we won't come close to making progress – not even if we work our way through the collected works of Chrysippus, with those of Antipater and Archedemus thrown in for good measure.

10
How to fight against impressions

[1] Every habit and faculty is formed or strengthened by the corresponding act – walking makes you walk better, running makes you a better runner. [2] If you want to be literate, read, if you want to be a painter, paint. Go a month without reading, occupied with something else, and you'll see what the result is. [3] And if you're laid up a mere ten days, when you get up and try to walk any distance you'll find your legs barely able to support you. [4] So if you like doing something, do it regularly; if you don't like doing something, make a habit of doing something different.

[5] The same goes for moral inclinations. When you get angry, you should know that you aren't guilty of an isolated lapse, you've encouraged a trend and thrown fuel on the fire. [6] When you can't resist sex with someone, don't think of it as a temporary setback; you've fed your weakness and made it harder to uproot. [7] It is inevitable that continuous behaviour of any one kind is going to instil new habits and tendencies, while steadily confirming old ones.

[8] And as philosophers point out, this, of course, is how moral infirmities develop also. If you are seized by greed on some occasion, reason can be invoked to alert you to the danger. Then the passion will abate and the mind will be restored to its former balance. [9] But if you

don't bring anything by way of relief, the mind will not return to normal; when it's inflamed by an impression, it will yield to passion more quickly the next time. Keep it up, and the mind grows inured to vice; eventually the love of money is entrenched. [10] When someone contracts smallpox, if he lives he is not the same as he was before the illness, unless the recovery is complete. [11] It's the same with the passions of the soul; they leave certain scars and blisters behind. And unless you remove them well, the next time you're flogged on the same spot those blisters will be open wounds.

[12] So if you don't want to be cantankerous, don't feed your temper, or multiply incidents of anger. Suppress the first impulse to be angry, then begin to count the days on which you don't get mad. [13] 'I used to be angry every day, then only every other day, then every third . . .' If you resist it a whole month, offer God a sacrifice, because the vice begins to weaken from day one, until it is wiped out altogether. [14] 'I didn't lose my temper this day, or the next, and not for two, then three months in succession.' If you can say that, you are now in excellent health, believe me.

[15] Today, when I saw a good-looking girl, I didn't say to myself, 'It would be nice to sleep with her,' or 'Her husband's one lucky guy.' Because that's tantamount to saying, 'Anyone would be lucky to sleep with her, even in adultery.' [16] Nor do I fantasize about what comes next – the woman undressing in front of me, then joining me in bed. [17] I pat myself on the back and say, 'Well done, Epictetus, you've solved a devilishly difficult problem, much harder than the Master Argument itself.' [18] But if

the woman is willing, if she calls to me or gives me a nod, if she takes me by the arm, and begins to rub up against me – and still I overcome my lust – well, that's a test far harder than the Liar paradox, it even beats the Quiescent. That's the sort of thing to boast about – not propounding the Master.

[19] So how does one get there? Start by wanting to please yourself, for a change, and appear worthy in the eyes of God. Desire to become pure, and, once pure, you will be at ease with yourself, and comfortable in the company of God. [20] Then, as Plato said, when a dangerous impression confronts you, go and expiate the gods with sacrifice, go to the temples to supplicate the gods for protection. [21] It will even do to socialize with men of good character, in order to model your life on theirs, whether you choose someone living or someone from the past.

[22] Consider Socrates; look how he lay next to Alcibiades and merely teased him about his youthful beauty. Think how proud he must have been to have won that victory over himself – an Olympic-sized victory, and one worthy of a successor to Heracles; so, really, he's the one who deserves to be addressed, 'Greetings, hero' – not these grimy boxers and pancratiasts or gladiators, their current counterparts.

[23] With these thoughts to defend you, you should triumph over any impression and not be dragged away. [24] Don't let the force of the impression when first it hits you knock you off your feet; just say to it, 'Hold on a moment; let me see who you are and what you represent. Let me put you to the test.' Next, don't let it pull you in by picturing to yourself the pleasures that await you.

[25] Otherwise it will lead you by the nose wherever it wants. Oppose it with some good and honourable thought, and put the dirty one to rout. [26] Practise this regularly, and you'll see what shoulders, what muscles, what stamina you acquire. Today people care only for academic discussion, nothing beyond that. [27] But I'm presenting to you the real athlete, namely the one training to face off against the most formidable of impressions.

Steady now, poor man, don't let impressions sweep you off your feet. [28] It's a great battle, and God's work. It's a fight for autonomy, freedom, happiness and peace. [29] Remember God, ask him to be your helper and protector, as sailors pray to the Dioscuri for help in a storm. Is there any storm greater than the storm of forceful impressions that can put reason to flight? What is a real storm except just another impression? [30] Put away the fear of death, and however much thunder and lightning you have to face, you will find the mind capable of remaining calm and composed regardless.

[31] If you lose the struggle once, but insist that next time it will be different, then repeat the same routine – be sure that in the end you will be in so sad and weakened a condition that you won't even realize your mistakes, you'll begin to rationalize your misbehaviour. [32] You will be living testimony to Hesiod's verse:

'Make a bad beginning and you'll contend with troubles ever after.'

II

What is the material proper to the good person and what is the goal they should strive to achieve

[1] The body is the raw material of the doctor and physical therapist. Land is the farmer's raw material. The raw material of the good man is his mind – his goal being to respond to impressions the way nature intended. [2] As a general rule, nature designed the mind to assent to what is true, dissent from what is false and suspend judgement in doubtful cases. Similarly, it conditioned the mind to desire what is good, to reject what is bad and to regard with indifference what is neither one nor the other. [3] Just as it is not in the power of a banker or retailer to reject Caesar's money – they are forced to make a proportional exchange whether they want to or not – so it is with the soul: [4] when presented with something good it gravitates towards it immediately, as it recoils from anything bad. The soul will never reject a clear impression of good, any more than Caesar's coin can be refused. The actions of gods as well as men are entirely based on this principle.

[5] It follows that the good is preferred over every human association. I care nothing for my father – only for the good.

'Are you that unfeeling?'

I am that way designed; it is the currency God gave me.

[6] The upshot is that, if the good turns out to be something other than decency and fairness, then father, brother, country and the rest can all go hang. [7] Now look, am I supposed to step aside and abandon my good just so you can have yours? Why?

'Because I'm your father.'

But not the good.

'I'm your brother.'

But not the good.

[8] If, however, we locate the good in soundness of character, then it becomes good to maintain these relationships. Whoever gives up some material things also wins the good.

[9] 'My father is laying waste to my inheritance.'

But not harming you.

'My brother will claim more than his share.'

He's welcome to as much as he likes. Will he take a greater share of honesty, loyalty and brotherly love? [10] No; even Zeus cannot deprive you of that fortune – because he chose not to be able to. He entrusted it to me and gave me a share equal to his own – free, clear and unencumbered.

[11] If people have a different currency, just flash it, and whatever is for sale there will be yours in exchange. [12] A corrupt governor has come to power in our province. What currency does he recognize? Silver. Show him silver, then, and you can cart off what you like. Here is an adulterer. His currency takes the form of pretty girls. 'Take the money, and sell me the merchandise.' In this

way they are bought and sold. [13] Here is one whose taste runs to boys. Procure him his currency and you can take what you please. Another is devoted to the hunt. Offer him some handsome horse or dog, and he will groan and complain, but in the end sell off whatever he has in order to make your price. You see, another from within forces him to act like this, ever since he designated this his currency.

[14] Here is the primary means of training yourself: as soon as you leave in the morning, subject whatever you see or hear to close study. Then formulate answers as if they were posing questions. Today what did you see – some beautiful woman or handsome man? Test them by your rule – does their beauty have any bearing on your character? If not, forget them. What else did you see? [15] Someone in mourning for the death of a child? Apply your rule. Death too is indifferent, so dismiss it from your mind. A consul crossed your path; apply your rule. What category of thing is a consulship – a good of the mind or one of matter? If it's the latter, then out with it, it failed our test. If it is nothing to you, reject it.

[16] Now, if we continued to practise this discipline every day from morning to night, we would see some results, by God. [17] As it is, though, we are overcome by every impression that we meet. Only in school – if even there – does our brain briefly come to life. Outside school, whenever we see a person in mourning, we think to ourselves, 'She's crushed.' If we happen to spy a consul, we think, 'There goes one lucky man.' The sight of a person in exile elicits 'How tragic' in response; a beggar prompts us to think, 'Poor guy, he doesn't even have money

enough for food.' [18] These are the insidious opinions we need to concentrate hard to expunge. What, after all, are sighing and crying, except opinions? What is 'misfortune'? An opinion. And sectarian strife, dissension, blame and accusation, ranting and raving – [19] they all are mere opinion, the opinion that good and bad lie outside us. Let someone transfer these opinions to the workings of the will, and I personally guarantee his peace of mind, no matter what his outward circumstances are like.

[20] The soul is like a bowl of water, with the soul's impressions like the rays of light that strike the water. [21] Now, if the water is disturbed, the light appears to be disturbed together with it – though of course it is not. [22] So when someone loses consciousness, it is not the person's knowledge and virtues that are impaired, it is the breath that contains them. Once the breath returns to normal, knowledge and the virtues are restored to normal also.

12
Every circumstance represents an opportunity

[1] Just about everyone agrees that 'good' or 'bad' in the case of objective judgements applies to us, not to things outside us. [2] No one calls 'good' the fact that it is day, or 'bad' that it is night, or 'the greatest of evils' that three is equal to four. [3] No, they call correct judgement good and incorrect judgement bad – the consequence being that good even comes of error, when we recognize the error as such.

[4] And so it should be in life. 'Being healthy is good, being sick is bad.' No, my friend: enjoying health in the right way is good; making bad use of your health is bad. 'So even illness can benefit us?' [5] Why not, if even death and disability can? It was no small advantage Menoeceus derived from his dying, after all. 'Whoever says so is welcome to the same advantages!' Come, by his sacrifice didn't he save himself – that is, the patriot in him, the benefactor, the man of honour, the man of his word – all of whom would have died had he survived? [6] Conversely, he would have acquired the reputation for being timid, mean, treacherous and weak.

Well – do you think his death did him hardly any good? [7] I suppose the father of Admetus greatly enjoyed living on such base and despicable terms, [8] who afterward died all the same. For God's sake, stop honouring externals, quit turning yourself into the tool of mere matter, or of people who can supply you or deny you those material things. [9] So is it possible to benefit from these circumstances? Yes, from *every* circumstance, even abuse and slander. A boxer derives the greatest advantage from his sparring partner – and my accuser is my sparring partner. He trains me in patience, civility and even temper. [10] I mean, a doctor who puts me in a headlock and sets a dislocated pelvis or shoulder – he benefits me, however painful the procedure. So too does a trainer when he commands me to 'lift the weight with both your hands' – and the heavier it is, the greater the benefit to me.

Well, if someone trains me to be even-tempered, am I not benefited in that case? [11] This shows you do not know how to be helped by your fellow man. I have a bad neighbour – bad, that is, for himself. For me, though, he is good: he exercises my powers of fairness and sociability. A bad father, likewise, is bad for himself, but for me represents a blessing. [12] The wand of Hermes promises that 'whatever you touch will turn to gold'. For my part, I can say, 'bring what challenge you please and I will turn it to good account: bring illness, death, poverty, slander, a judgement of death: they will all be converted to advantage by my wand of Hermes.'

[13] 'What good will you get from death?'

'I will make it your glory, or the occasion for you to show how a person obeys the will of nature.'

[14] 'What will you make of illness?'

'I will expose its true nature by outdoing myself in calmness and serenity; I will neither beg the doctor's help, nor pray for death. [15] What more could you ask? Everything, you see, that you throw at me I will transform into a blessing, a boon – something dignified, even enviable.'

[16] But no. Instead, you say, 'Be careful that you don't get ill: it's bad.' Which is like saying, 'Guard against ever entertaining the idea that three is equivalent to four: it's bad.' How is it bad? If I weigh the statement correctly, what harm can it do me? It is more likely to help. [17] Similarly, it is enough if I hold the right idea about poverty, illness and removal from office: all such challenges will only serve my turn. No more, then, should I look for bad, and good, in external conditions.

[18] Ah, but these principles never leave the school, no one takes them with him when he goes back home. Instead, war immediately breaks out – with your slave, your neighbours, with people who scoff at these principles and make fun of you. [19] For my part, I bless Lesbios for daily reminding me that I know nothing.

13
On freedom

[1] Free is the person who lives as he wishes and cannot be coerced, impeded or compelled, whose impulses cannot be thwarted, who always gets what he desires and never has to experience what he would rather avoid.

Now, who would want to go through life ignorant of how to achieve this?

'No one.'

[2] Who wants to live with delusion and prejudice, being unjust, undisciplined, mean and ungrateful?

'No one.'

[3] No bad person, then, lives the way he wants, and no bad man is free. [4] Who wants to live life experiencing sadness, envy and pity, being frustrated in their desires and liable to experience what they want to avoid?

'No one.'

[5] So, can we find any bad person who is without sadness, fear, frustration or misfortune?

'No.'

No more, then, can we find one who is free.

[6] Now, a two-term consul will tolerate such talk only on condition that you add, 'But you know that already; it hardly applies to *you*.' If you tell him the truth and say, [7] 'You're just as much enslaved as someone sold into captivity three times over,' don't expect anything but a punch in the nose. 'How am *I* a slave?' he wants to know.

[8] 'My father is free, my mother is free, and there is no deed of sale for *me*. Add to which I'm a senator, I'm a personal friend of Caesar, I've been a consul and I own many slaves personally.' [9] In the first place, Senator, sir, your father could have been slavish in the same respect as you, along with your mother, your grandfather and all your ancestors down the line. [10] And even if they were as free as free can be, what does that have to do with you? Suppose that they were noble, and you are depraved? Or that they were courageous, whereas you are a coward? Or that they were disciplined, while you are dissolute?

[11] 'What's that got to do with being a slave?'

Doesn't it seem to you that acting against one's will, under protest and compulsion, is tantamount to being a slave?

[12] 'Maybe, but who has power to compel me except Caesar, who rules over everyone?'

[13] So you admit that you have at least one master. And don't let the fact that Caesar rules over everyone, as you say, console you: it only means that you're a slave in a very large household. [14] You remind me of the citizens of Nicopolis, who are forever proclaiming, 'By the grace of Caesar, we are free.'

[15] If you like, however, for the moment we'll leave Caesar out of account. Just tell me this: haven't you ever been in love with someone, be they man or woman, slave or free?

[16] 'How does that affect whether I am slave or free?'

[17] Weren't you ever commanded by your sweetheart to do something you didn't want to do? Did you never flatter your pet slave, and even kiss her feet? And yet if

someone were to force you to kiss Caesar's feet, you'd regard it as hubris and the height of tyranny.

[18] If your lovesick condition isn't slavery, then what is? Didn't you ever risk going out at night where you didn't want to go, spend more money than you had intended, say things in the course of the evening in accents of misery and woe, put up with being mocked, and finally locked out? [19] If you're too embarrassed to share your own experience, though, just consider the words and actions of Thrasonides, who fought more campaigns perhaps, than you. To begin with, he went out at a time of night that even his slave wouldn't dare do, or if forced to, only with much moaning and groaning about his bitter condition. [20] And what does Thrasonides say? 'A pretty woman has made of me a perfect slave, something not even my fiercest enemies could accomplish.' [21] Poor guy, to be enslaved to a whore, and a cheap one at that! What right do you still have to call yourself free? What point is there in boasting about your military victories?

[22] Then the man calls for a sword to end it all, yells at the slave who refuses to give him one out of compassion, sends gifts to his girl – who still despises him – begs and implores her and rejoices when he meets with the least success. [23] But until he succeeds in suppressing his lust and anxiety, how is he really free?

[24] Consider how we apply the idea of freedom to animals. [25] There are tame lions that people cage, raise, feed and take with them wherever they go. Yet who will call such a lion free? The easier its life, the more slavish it is. No lion endowed with reason and discretion would choose to be one of these pet specimens.

[26] The birds above us, when they are caught and raised in a cage, will try anything for the sake of escape. Some starve to death rather than endure their condition. [27] Those that survive – barely, grudgingly, wasting away – fly off in an instant when they find the least little opening to squeeze through, so great is their need for their native freedom, so strong the desire to be independent and unconfined. [28] 'Well, what's wrong with you here in your cage?' 'You can ask? I was born to fly wherever I like, to live in the open air, to sing whenever I want. You take all this away from me and then say, "What's wrong with you?"'

[29] For this reason we will only call those animals free that refuse to tolerate captivity and escape instead by dying as soon as they are caught. [30] Apropos of which, Diogenes says somewhere that one way to guarantee freedom is to be ready to die. To the Persian king he wrote, 'You can no more make slaves of the Athenians than you can make slaves of the fish of the sea.' [31] 'Why? Can't Athenians be captured?' 'Capture them, and straight away they'll give you the slip and be gone, like fish, which die directly they are caught and taken on board. And if the Athenians die when taken captive, what good in the end is all your military might?' [32] There's the word of a free man who has given the subject of freedom considerable thought and, sure enough, discovered the real meaning of the word. If you continue to look for it in the wrong place, however, don't be surprised if you never find it.

[33] The slave urgently prays to be emancipated. Why? Do you suppose it's because he can't wait to pay the tax

collector the five per cent tax? No, it's because he ima-gines that, lacking liberty, he's been thwarted and unhappy all his life up to then. [34] 'Once I'm set free,' he says, 'everything will be roses right away. I won't have to wait on anybody, I can talk to everyone as an equal and a peer, travel wherever I like, come and go as I please.'

[35] Then he is liberated, but now, lacking a place to eat, he looks around for someone to sweet-talk and dine with. Next he resorts to prostitution and, if he gets a sugar daddy, he suffers the most degrading fate of all, having now fallen into a far more abject slavery than the one he escaped. [36] Even if he succeeds on his own, his low breeding makes him fall in love with a common pros-titute. When she refuses him he falls apart and longs to be a slave again.

[37] 'What did I lack then, anyway? Another person supplied me with clothes, shoes and food and took care of me when I was sick; and I had little enough to do by way of service in return. Now I go through hell catering to many people instead of just the one. [38] Still – if I can only manage to get a ring on my finger, then finally my life will be blissful and complete.' Well, to get it he has to endure the usual humiliations; and once he has it, it's the same old story again.

[39] So then he thinks: 'If I serve a stint in the military all my troubles will be over.' Consequently he joins the army, suffers everything a rank-and-file soldier has to suffer, and enlists for a second and then a third tour of duty. [40] Finally, when he crowns it off by becoming a senator, then he becomes a slave in fine company, then he experiences the poshest and most prestigious form of enslavement.

[41] No more foolishness. The man has to learn 'what each specific thing means', as Socrates often said, and stop casually applying preconceptions to individual cases. [42] This is the cause of everyone's troubles, the inability to apply common preconceptions to particulars. Instead the opinions of men as to what is bad diverge. [43] One thinks that he is unwell, when it's nothing of the kind; the problem is that he is not adapting preconceptions correctly. One imagines that he is poor, another that he has a difficult mother or father, still another that Caesar is not disposed in his favour. This is all caused by one and the same thing, namely, ignorance of how to apply one's preconceptions.

[44] Who, after all, does not have a preconception of 'bad', to the effect that it is harmful, that it should be avoided, and that we should use every means to get rid of it? One preconception does not conflict with another, [45] conflict arises when it comes to their application. What is this 'bad', then, which is also harmful and needs to be avoided? One says it's not being Caesar's friend: he's off the mark, he's not applying preconceptions properly, and is distressed because he's stuck on something that doesn't meet the definition. Because if he succeeds in securing Caesar's friendship he still hasn't got what he wants – [46] the same thing, really, that we all want: to live in peace, to be happy, to do as we like and never be foiled or forced to act against our wishes.

When a man gains Caesar's friendship, does he stop being hindered or constrained, does he live in peace and happiness? Whom should we ask? Well, who is more to be trusted than the person who has actually gained his confidence? [47] So step up, sir, and tell us, when did you sleep more soundly, now or before you became intimate with Caesar? 'By the gods, stop mocking my condition. You don't know what agonies I endure. I can't even fall off to sleep before someone comes and announces, "The emperor is up already, and about to make his appearance," and then I'm harassed by one worry and crisis after another.'

[48] Well, and when did you dine with greater contentment, now or earlier? Hear him testify to this, too. He says that if he's not invited to dine with Caesar, he's an emotional wreck; and if he is invited, he behaves like a slave asked to sit beside his master, anxious the whole time lest he say or do something gauche. But is he afraid that, like a slave, he'll get whipped? He should be so lucky. As befits a personage as lofty as a friend of Caesar, he's afraid his head will be chopped off.

[49] When did you bathe with more ease, when were you more relaxed at your exercise – in a word, which life would you prefer, the present or the previous one? [50] I could swear that there is no one so crude or forgetful that they don't actually regret their fortune in precise proportion to how close to Caesar they've become.

[51] Well, if neither kings, so-called, nor their companions live as they please, who is left that can be considered free? Look and you will find: nature has endowed you with resources to discover the truth. And if you can't infer the answer yourself using only these resources, [52] listen to what those who have explored the question have to say:

'Do you think freedom is something good?'

'The greatest good of all.'

'Can anyone in possession of the greatest good be unhappy or unfortunate?'

'No.'

'Anyone you see who is unhappy, then, malcontent or disheartened, you can confidently characterize as not being free?'

'Yes.'

[53] Now we have surely advanced beyond consideration of buying, selling and other such mundane transactions. Because if you were right to agree to what we said above, then if he is unhappy the Great King himself cannot be free, nor can any prince, consul or two-term consul.

'Granted.'

[54] Well, then, answer me something else: do you think freedom is grand and glorious, a thing of some significance?

'Of course.'

And can anyone possessed of something so grand, glorious and important feel inferior?

'Impossible.'

[55] Then whenever you see someone grovel before another, or flatter them insincerely, you can safely assume that that person is not free – and not just if a meal is at stake, but even when they abase themselves for the sake of a governorship or consulship. In fact, you can call the people who behave that way for small gains petty slaves, while the latter deserve to be called slaves on a grand scale.

[56] 'I would have to agree with that too.'

And do you think of freedom as something autonomous and self-sufficient?

'Yes.'

Then whoever is liable to be hindered or compelled by someone else is assuredly not free. [57] And please don't research the status of their grandfather and great-grandfather, or inquire into whether they were bought or sold. If you hear someone say 'Master' sincerely and with feeling, call him a slave no matter if twelve body-guards march ahead of him. Or if you hear, 'God, the things I put up with!', call the person a slave. If you just see him disconsolate, angry or out of sorts, call him a slave – albeit a slave in a purple toga.

[58] Even if he does none of these things, don't call him free just yet, acquaint yourself with his judgements, in case they show any sign of constraint, disappointment or disaffection. And if you find him so disposed, call him a slave on holiday at the Saturnalia. Say that his master is away; when he returns, the man's true condition will be made plain to you.

[59] 'When who returns?'

Whoever has the means to give or take away any of the things he values.

'Do we have that many masters?'

We do. Because over and above the rest we have masters in the form of circumstances, which are legion. And anyone who controls any one of them controls us as well. [60] No one, you realize, fears Caesar himself, it is death, exile, dispossession, jail and disenfranchisement that they are afraid of. Nor is Caesar loved, unless by chance he is personally deserving; we love money, a tribuneship, a military command or consulship. But when we love, hate or fear such things, then the people who administer them are bound to become our masters. [61] As a result we even honour them as gods, because we associate godhead with whatever has the capacity to confer most benefit. Then we posit a false minor premise: *this* man has the power to confer the most benefit. And the conclusion that follows from these premises is necessarily false as well.

[62] What is it then that renders a person free and independent? Money is not the answer, nor is a governorship, a consulship, or even a kingdom. [63] Something else needs to be found. Well, what makes for freedom and fluency in the practice of writing? Knowledge of how to write. The same goes for the practice of playing an instrument. It follows that, in the conduct of life, there must be a science to living well. [64] Now, you have heard this stated as a general principle, consider how it is borne out in particular cases. Take someone in want of something under the control of people other than himself; is it possible for him to be unrestricted or unrestrained?

'No.'

[65] Consequently he cannot be free either. Now consider: is there nothing that is under our control, is *everything* under our control – or are there some things we control, and others that we don't?

'What do you mean?'

[66] Is it within your power to have your body perform perfectly whenever you want?

'No.'

Or be in good health?

'No.'

Or attractive?

'Again, no.'

Well, then, the body isn't yours, and is subject to everything physically stronger.

'Granted.'

[67] What about land – can you have as much as you want, for as long as you want, in the condition you prefer?

'No.'

And what about slaves?

'No again.'

Clothing?

'No.'

Your house?

'No.'

Your horses?

'No to all of the above.'

And if more than anything else you want your children to live, or your wife, your brother, or your friends, is this within your power to effect?

'No, that isn't either.'

[68] Is there nothing that is under your authority, that you have exclusive control over – does anything of the kind exist?

'I don't know.'

[69] Well, look at it this way. Can anyone make you assent to a false proposition?

'No, no one can.'

So in the field of assent you cannot be hindered or obstructed.

'Evidently.'

[70] And can anyone force you to choose something to which you're opposed?

'They can: when they threaten me with death or imprisonment, they compel my choice.'

But what if you despise death and imprisonment – are you still in that person's thrall?

'No.'

[71] Is your attitude towards death your affair, then?

'It is.'

Therefore your will is your own business too.

'I grant it.'

And that goes for being opposed to something, also.

[72] 'But suppose I choose to walk, and someone obstructs me?'

What part of you will they obstruct? Certainly not your power of assent?

'No, my body.'

Your body, yes – as they might obstruct a rock.

'Perhaps; but the upshot is, now I'm not allowed to walk.'

[73] Whoever told you, 'Walking is your irrevocable privilege'? I said only that the will to walk could not be obstructed. Where use of the body and its cooperation are concerned, you've long been told that that isn't your responsibility.

[74] 'Very well.'

And can you be forced by anyone to desire something against your will?

'No.'

Or to plan for, or project – or, in a word, regard outside impressions in any one way at all?

[75] 'No again. But when I've already conceived a wish for something, they can stop me from getting it.'

If you wish for something that is under your authority and cannot be obstructed, how will they stop you?

'They can't.'

And who says if you desire something outside your authority that you cannot be obstructed?

[76] 'Well, should I not desire health, then?'

No – nor, for that matter, anything else outside the limits of your authority; [77] and whatever you cannot produce or preserve at will lies outside your range. Don't let your hands go near it, much less your desire. Otherwise you've consigned yourself to slavery and submitted your neck to the yoke, as you do whenever you prize something not yours to command, or grow attached to something like health that's contingent on God's will and variable, unstable, unpredictable and unreliable by nature.

[78] 'So my arm isn't mine either?'

It's a part of you, but by nature it is dirt, subject to restraint and main force, a slave to anything physically stronger. [79] And why single the arm out? For as long as its time lasts the whole body should be treated like a loaded donkey. If a donkey is requisitioned and seized by a soldier, let it go: don't resist or complain, or you'll be beaten, and lose the animal all the same. [80] And if this is how you should treat the body, what treatment should be reserved for the things that serve the body? If it's a donkey, then they are the donkey's bridle, pack saddle, shoes, barley and feed. Let them go too, give them up with even more speed and good grace than you did the animal.

[81] When you're thus practised and prepared to discriminate between what belongs to you and what doesn't, what is subject to hindrance and what is not, and are ready to regard the latter as important to you and the former as irrelevant, then is there anyone, any more, you need be frightened of?

'No.'

[82] No; because what would you fear them *for*? Not the things that are your own, that constitute the essence of what is good and bad, because no one has power over them but you. You can no more be blocked or deprived of them than can God. [83] Perhaps you fear for the body and material possessions – things that lie outside your scope of responsibility and have no meaning for you. But what else have you been doing from the start except distinguishing between what you own and what you don't, between what is in your power and what is not, between what is subject to hindrance and what isn't? Why else have you been frequenting philosophers? So that you could be as lost and unhappy as you were before? [84] In that case you will never be free of fear or anxiety – or sorrow, which does you no credit either, seeing as fear for future evils turns to sorrow when they turn up.

Nor should you feel irrational desire any more. You have a fixed and measured desire for the goods of the soul, since they are within your power and accessible. You disdain external goods, so that no opening exists for that irrational, intemperate and impulsive form of desire. [85] With such an attitude towards things, you can no longer be intimidated by anyone. What can one human being find strange or frightful in a fellow human's appearance, conversation or companionship generally? Nothing – any more than one horse, or dog, or bee is frightening to another of its kind. People find particular things, however, frightening; and it's when someone is able to threaten or entice us with those that the man himself becomes frightening.

[86] How is a fortress demolished? Not with weapons or fire – with judgements. We can capture the physical fortress, the one in the city, but our judgements about illness, or about attractive women, remain to be dislodged from the fortress inside us, together with the tyrants whom we host every day, though their identities change over time. [87] It's here that we need to start attacking the fortress and driving the tyrants out. Surrender the body and its members, physical faculties, property, reputation, office, honours, children, siblings – repudiate them all. [88] And if the tyrants are expelled from it, the fortress itself will not have to be destroyed, not at least as far as I'm concerned. For it does me no harm while it stands.

The tyrants' bodyguards, too, can stay, for how can they affect me? Their sticks, their spears and their knives are meant for other people. [89] I, personally, was never kept from something I wanted, nor had forced upon me something I was opposed to. How did I manage it? I submitted my will to God. He wants me to be sick – well, then, so do I. He wants me to choose something. Then I choose it. He wants me to desire something, I desire it. He wants me to get something, I want the same; or he doesn't want me to get it, and I concur. [90] Thus I even assent to death and torture. Now no one can make me, or keep me, from acting in line with my inclination, any more than they can similarly manipulate God.

[91] This is the way circumspect travellers act. Word reaches them that the road is beset with highwaymen. A solitary traveller doesn't like the odds, he waits in order to attach himself to an ambassador, quaestor or provincial governor and only travels securely once he's part of their entourage. [92] Which is how a prudent person proceeds along life's road. He thinks, 'There are countless thieves and bandits, many storms, and many chances to get lost or relieved of one's belongings. [93] How are we to evade them and come through without being attacked? [94] What party should we wait to join, with whom should we enlist, to ensure safe passage? With this man, perhaps – the person who is rich and influential? No, not much to be gained there; he's liable to lose his position, break down and prove of no use to me at all. And suppose my travel companion himself betrays and robs me?

[95] 'Well, then, I'll become a friend of Caesar – no one will try to take advantage of me as long as I am Caesar's friend. But in the first place, what will I need to suffer or sacrifice in order to get close to him? How much money will I have to spend, on how many people? [96] And if I do manage it – well, after all, the emperor is mortal too. Add to which, if by some mischance he becomes my enemy, I suppose I will have no recourse except to flee and take refuge in the wilderness. [97] But what about illness – I can't escape that in the wilderness. So what remains? Is no travel companion dependable, honest and above suspicion?'

[98] By a process of logical elimination, the conclusion emerges that we will come through safely only by allying ourselves with God.

[99] 'What do you mean, "allying ourselves"?'

Acting in such a way that, whatever God wants, we want too; and by inversion whatever he does *not* want, this we do not want either. [100] How can we do this? By paying attention to the pattern of God's purpose and design. To start with, then, what has he given me as mine outright, and what has he reserved to himself? He has conferred on me the functions of the will, made them mine and made them proof against resistance or obstruction. But the body, which is made of clay – how could he make that unconstrained? So he assigned it its place in the cosmic cycle – the same as other material things like my furniture, my house, my wife and children.

[101] So don't go up against God by hoping for what is unattainable, namely to keep for ever what doesn't really belong to you. Keep them in the spirit they were given, for as long as possible. If he gives he also takes away. So why try and resist him? It would be stupid to oppose one who is stronger than I, but more importantly, it would be wrong. [102] For how did I come by these belongings in the first place? From my father – who got them from his. Who created the sun, though, the fruits of the earth, and the seasons? Who engineered mankind's mutual attraction, and the social order?

[103] When everything you have has been given you, including your very existence, you proceed to turn on your benefactor and fault him for taking things back. [104] Who are you, and how did you get here? It was God brought you into the world, who showed you the light, gave you the people who support you, gave you reason and perception. And he brought you into the world as a

mortal, to pass your time on earth with a little endowment of flesh, to witness his design and share for a short time in his feast and celebration. [105] So why not enjoy the feast and pageant while it's given you to do so; then, when he ushers you out, go with thanks and reverence for what you were privileged for a time to see and hear.

'No, I want to keep celebrating.'

[106] Yes, just as initiates want the mysteries to continue, or crowds at the Olympic Games want to see more contestants. But the festival is over; leave and move on, grateful for what you've seen, with your self-respect intact. Make room for other people, it's their turn to be born, just as you were born, and once born they need a place to live, along with the other necessities of life. If the first people won't step aside, what's going to happen? Don't be so greedy. Aren't you ever satisfied? Are you determined to make the world more crowded still?

[107] 'All right; but I'd like my wife and children to remain with me.'

Why? Are they yours? They belong to the one who gave them to you, the same one who created you. Don't presume to take what isn't yours, or oppose one who is your better.

[108] 'Why did he bring me into the world on these conditions?'

If the conditions don't suit you, leave. He doesn't need a heckler in the audience. He wants people keen to participate in the dance and revels – people, that is, who would sooner applaud and favour the festival with their praise and acclamation. [109] As for those who are grumpy and dour, he won't be sad to see them excluded. Even when they are invited, they don't act as if they are on holiday, or play an appropriate part; instead they whine, they curse their fate, their luck and their company. They don't appreciate what they have, including moral resources given to them for the opposite purpose – generosity of spirit, high-mindedness, courage and that very freedom we are now exploring.

[110] 'What did I get externals for, then?'

To use.

'For how long?'

For as long as the one who gave them decides.

'And if I can't live without them?'

Don't get attached to them and they won't be. Don't tell yourself that they're indispensable and they aren't.

[111] Those are the reflections you should recur to morning and night. Start with things that are least valuable and most liable to be lost – things such as a jug or a glass – and proceed to apply the same ideas to clothes, pets, livestock, property; then to yourself, your body, the body's parts, your children, your siblings and your wife. [112] Look on every side and mentally discard them. Purify your thoughts, in case of an attachment or devotion to something that doesn't belong to you and will hurt to have wrenched away. [113] And as you exercise daily, as you do at the gym, do not say that you are philosophizing (admittedly a pretentious claim), but that you are a slave presenting your emancipator; because this is genuine freedom that you cultivate.

[114] This is the kind of freedom Diogenes got from Antisthenes, saying he could never again be enslaved by anyone. [115] Which explains his behaviour towards the

pirates when they took him captive. Did he call any of them 'master'? No. And I don't mean the word; it's not the word I'm concerned with, but the attitude behind it. [116] He yelled at them for not feeding their captives better. And when he was sold, it was not a master he looked to get, but a slave of his own.

And how did he act towards his new owner? He at once began to criticize him, saying that he shouldn't dress this way, shouldn't cut his hair that way – besides advising him on how his sons should be brought up. [117] And why not? If the owner had bought a personal trainer, he would have acknowledged the trainer to be his superior, not his slave, so far as exercise is concerned. The same goes if he had bought a doctor or architect. In any field you care to name, the person with experience should command the one without. [118] So whoever is possessed of knowledge about how to live should naturally take precedence there. For who else is master of a ship except the captain? Why? Just because whoever disobeys him is punished?

[119] 'But so-and-so can have me whipped.'

Not with impunity, however.

'Well, so I believed too.'

And because he does not act with impunity, he does not act with authority; no one can get away with injustice.

[120] 'And what punishment do you foresee for the master who puts his own slave in chains?'

The act itself of putting him in chains – an idea even you will accept if you have any wish to honour the principle that human beings are civilized animals, not beasts. [121] A plant or animal fares poorly when it acts contrary to its nature; [122] and a human being is no different.

Well, then, biting, kicking, wanton imprisonment and beheading – is that what our nature entails? No; rather, acts of kindness, cooperation and good will. And so, whether you like it or not, a person fares poorly whenever he acts like an insensitive brute.

[123] 'So you're saying that Socrates did not fare poorly?'

That's right – the jurors and his accusers did instead.

'Nor Helvidius at Rome?'

No – but the person who killed him did.

'How do you reckon that?'

[124] Well, you don't call a fighting cock that's bloodied but victorious unfortunate, but rather one who lost without receiving a scratch. And you don't yell 'Good dog!' at one that doesn't hunt or work; you do it when you see one panting, labouring, exhausted from the chase. [125] What's odd in asserting that what's bad for anything is what runs contrary to its nature? You say it for everything else, why make humanity the sole exception?

[126] Well, but we assert that in their nature human beings are gentle, honest and cooperative – that's pretty ridiculous, is it not? No, that isn't either – [127] which is why no one suffers harm even if they are flogged, jailed or beheaded. The victim may be majestic in suffering, you see, and come through a better, more fortunate person; while the one who really comes to harm, who suffers the most and the most pitifully, is the person who is transformed from human being to wolf, snake or hornet.

[128] All right then, let us go over the points we are agreed on. The unhindered person is free, that is, the person who has ready access to things in the condition he

prefers. Whoever can be thwarted, however, or coerced, frustrated or forced into a situation against their will – that person is a slave. [129] The person who renounces externals cannot be hindered, as externals are things that are not within our power either to have or not to have – or to have in the condition we might like. [130] Externals include the body and its members, as well as material goods. If you grow attached to any of them as if they were your own, you will incur the penalties prescribed for a thief.

[131] This is the road that leads to liberty, the only road that delivers us from slavery: finally to be able to say, with meaning:

Lead me, Zeus, lead me, Destiny,

to the goal I was long ago assigned.

[132] What about you, philosopher? The tyrant is going to call on you to bear false witness. Tell us: do you play along or not?

'Let me think it over.'

Think it over *now*? What were you thinking over in school? Didn't you rehearse which things are good, which are bad, and which are neither?

[133] 'I did.'

And what did you decide?

'That justice and fairness are good, vice and injustice bad.'

Is life a good?

'No.'

Is dying bad?

'No.'

Or jail?

'No.'

And what about slanderous and dishonest talk, betraying a friend, and trying to ingratiate yourself with a tyrant – how exactly did you characterize those?

[134] 'As bad.'

Well, it's obvious that you aren't thinking it over, and you never did think it over in the past. I mean, how much thought is really required to decide whether you should exercise your power to get the greatest goods and avoid the greatest evils? A fit subject for thought, no doubt, calling for a great deal of deliberation. Who are you kidding? No such inquiry ever took place. [135] If you really did believe that vice alone is bad and everything else indifferent, you never would have needed time to 'think it over' – far from it. You'd be able to make a decision immediately, using your faculty of reason as readily as sight. [136] I mean, when do you have to 'think over' whether black things are white, or light things heavy? No, the clear evidence of the senses is enough. So why say now that you have to 'think over' whether indifferents are more to be avoided than evils? [137] The fact is, this is not what you really believe: you don't think that death and jail, etc. are indifferent, you count them among the greatest evils; and you don't regard false witness, etc. as evil, but matters of indifference.

[138] You've developed this habit from the beginning. 'Where am I? In school. And who is my audience? I'm conversing with philosophers. But now that I've left school, away with those pedantic and naive doctrines.' And thus a philosopher comes to traduce a friend, [139] thus a philosopher turns informer and prostitutes his principles, thus a

member of the Senate comes to betray his beliefs. Inside, his real opinion cries out to be heard – [140] no faint or timid idea, based on casual reasoning and hanging, as it were, by a thread, but a strong and vital conviction rooted in practical experience.

[141] Be careful how you take the news – I won't say that your child died, because you couldn't possibly tolerate that – but that your cruet of oil fell over. Or that someone drank up all your wine. [142] Anyone finding you in despair might well say, simply, 'Philosopher, you sang a different tune in school. Don't try to deceive us, or pretend that you are a human being when you're no more than a worm.' [143] I'd like to come upon one of them having sex, just to see how much they exert themselves and what kind of sounds they make; whether they remember who they are or recall any of the sentiments which they hear and preach and read.

[144] What has any of this to do with freedom? On the contrary, nothing *except* this relates to freedom, whether rich people such as you choose to believe it or not.

[145] 'What proof do you have of that?'

Only you yourselves, with your abject reverence for your great master, the emperor, whose every nod and gesture you live by. You faint if he even squints at you, and toady before the old men and women of the court, saying, 'I can't possibly do that, I'm not allowed.' [146] And why can't you? Weren't you just arguing with me that you were free? 'But Aprulla won't let me.' Tell the truth, slave – don't run away from your masters or refuse to acknowledge them, don't dare to invoke an emancipator when proofs of your servitude are so manifest.

[147] I mean, someone constrained by love to act against their better judgement, who sees the right thing to do but is powerless to act on it, might be considered the more deserving of compassion inasmuch as they are in the grip of a violent and, in some ways, a supernatural force. [148] But what sympathy can you expect with your passion for old men and women, as you wipe their nose and wash their face, ply them with presents and nurse them when they're sick as if you are their slave – all the while praying for their death and pestering their doctors to find out if they are terminal yet or not. Or when you kiss the hands of other people's slaves, making yourself the slave of slaves, all for the sake of these great and glorious honours and offices – what can you expect then?

[149] So don't parade before me in your pride because you are a consul or a praetor – I know how you came by these offices, and who presented them to you. [150] Speaking for myself, I would rather be dead than owe my living to Felicio, having to put up with his airs and his typical slave's impertinence. I know what a slave is like who has acquired influence and self-importance.

[151] 'Are *you* free, then?'

By God I wish I were, and I pray to be; but I still can't face my masters, I continue to value my poor body, I attach great importance to keeping healthy – though it isn't healthy at all. [152] But I *can* show you a free man, to satisfy your desire for an exemplar. Diogenes – he was free. Why? Not because his parents were free (they weren't), but because he himself was. He had eliminated any means to capture him, there was no opening to attack or seize him in order to make him a slave. [153] Everything he owned was disposable, and only temporarily attached. If you had seized any of his possessions, he would have surrendered it to you sooner than be pulled along behind it. If you had grabbed him by the leg, he would have given up the leg; if you had seized his entire body, the entire body would have been sacrificed. The same with family, friends and country: he knew where they had come from, from whom, and on what terms.

[154] His true parents – the gods – these he never would have dared sacrifice; nor his real country, the world at large. He yielded to no one in his zeal to serve and obey the gods, and there is no one who would have sooner died for his country. [155] He did not care for the mere appearance of acting on the world's behalf; he constantly bore in mind that events all have their source there and happen for the sake of that universal homeland by the command of God, who governs it. Observe, therefore, what he personally says and writes: [156] 'Here's why, Diogenes, you are at liberty to speak your mind to the Persian king as well as to Archidamus, king of the Spartans.' [157] Is it because he was of freeborn parentage? Sure, and I suppose the reason all the citizens of Athens, Sparta and Corinth could *not* address them as they pleased, but feared and flattered them instead, was that their parents all were slaves. [158] So why did he enjoy this licence? 'Because I don't consider the body to be my own, because I lack for nothing, and because the law is the only thing I esteem, nothing else.' That's what enabled him to be free.

[159] And just so you don't think I choose as my exemplar of freedom someone unencumbered by wife,

children, friends, relatives and the demands of citizenship, factors that could make one bend and compromise, take for consideration Socrates, who had both wife and children, but as if they were on loan. He had a country, to the degree and in the manner called for; he had friends and relatives – but all these were subordinate to the law and the need to obey it.

[160] And so, when he was drafted to serve, he was the first one to leave home, and once on the line fought without any regard for his life. Ordered by the tyrants to arrest Leon, he did not give a thought to obeying, because he thought the act unlawful, even knowing there was a chance he might die if he refused. [161] He didn't care; it was not his skin he wanted to save, but the man of honour and integrity. These things are not open to compromise or negotiation.

[162] Later, when he had to defend himself at risk of his life, he did not comport himself like someone with a wife and children, but as someone alone and unattached. And how did he behave when it was time to drink the poison? [163] Given the opportunity to save himself, with Crito urging him to go into exile for his children's sake, did he look upon this as the lucky pretext he needed to stay alive? Hardly. He reflected on the right thing to do, with no thought or regard for anything else. In his own words, he didn't want to save the body, he wanted to preserve the element that grows and thrives with every act of justice, the element that is diminished and dies by injustice. [164] Socrates does not save his life at the cost of dishonour – Socrates, who resisted the Athenians' call to bring an illegal motion to a vote, defied the tyrants, and

spoke so memorably on the subject of virtue and character. Such a man is not saved with dishonour; [165] an honourable death, not flight, is his salvation. A good actor preserves his reputation not by speaking lines out of turn but by knowing when to talk – and when to keep quiet.

[166] So what will become of his children? 'If I had run off to Thessaly, you would have cared for them. If I go to Hades, will no one be there to look after them?' Note how he makes light of death, and sports with the idea of it. [167] If it had been you or I, we quickly would have rationalized our behaviour thus: 'People who wrong us should be paid back in kind,' not failing to add, 'If my life is spared I will help many people, but dead I'm of no use to anyone.' If we had to squeeze through a mousehole to escape, we would have done it. [168] But how could we then have helped anyone, with our friends still back in Athens? If we had been helpful alive, wouldn't we have done people much more good by accepting death in the appropriate time and manner? [169] Even now, long after Socrates' death, the memory of what he did and said benefits humanity as much as or more than ever.

[170] Study this – these principles, these arguments – and contemplate these models of behaviour, if you want to be free, and your desire corresponds to the goal's importance. [171] Don't be surprised if so great a goal costs you many a sacrifice. For love of what they considered freedom men have hanged themselves, have thrown themselves over cliffs – and whole cities have occasionally been destroyed. [172] For true, inviolable, unassailable freedom, yield to God when he asks for something back that he earlier gave you. Prepare yourself, as Plato

says, not just for death, but for torture, exile, flogging – and the loss of everything not belonging to you. [173] You will be a slave among slaves otherwise; even if you are a consul ten thousand times over, even if you make your residence on the Palatine, you will be a slave none the less.

And you'll realize, as Cleanthes used to say, that what philosophers say may be contrary to expectation, but not to reason. [174] For you will learn by experience that it's true: the things that men admire and work so hard to get prove useless to them once they're theirs. Meanwhile people to whom such things are still denied come to imagine that everything good will be theirs if only they could acquire them. Then they get them: and their longing is unchanged, their anxiety is unchanged, their disgust is no less, and they still long for whatever is lacking. [175] Freedom is not achieved by satisfying desire, but by eliminating it. [176] Assure yourself of this by expending as much effort on these new ambitions as you did on those illusive goals: work day and night to attain a liberated frame of mind. [177] Instead of a rich old man, cultivate the company of a philosopher, be seen hanging around *his* door for a change. There's no shame in the association, and you won't go away unedified or empty-handed, provided you go with the right attitude. Try at least; there is no shame in making an honest effort.

14
On social intercourse

[1] You should be especially careful when associating with one of your former friends or acquaintances not to sink to their level; otherwise you will lose yourself. [2] If you are troubled by the idea that 'He'll think I'm boring and won't treat me the way he used to,' remember that everything comes at a price. It isn't possible to change your behaviour and still be the same person you were before.

[3] So choose: either regain the love of your old friends by reverting to your former self or remain better than you once were and forfeit their affection. [4] And if you choose the latter, stick to it from here on out. Don't give in to second thoughts, because no one who wavers will make progress. And if you are committed to making progress and ready to devote yourself to the effort, then give up everything else. [5] Otherwise your ambivalence will only ensure that you don't make progress, and you won't even get to revisit the pleasures of the past.

[6] Formerly, when you were devoted to worthless pursuits, your friends found you congenial company. [7] But you can't be a hit in both roles. To the extent you cultivate one you will fall short in the other. You can't seem as affable to your old cronies if you don't go out drinking with them as of old. So choose whether you want to be a charming drunk in their company, or dull and sober on your own. You can't expect the same recep-

tion from the group you used to associate with if you don't go carousing with them regularly any more.

So again you have a choice: [8] if you value dignity and restraint over being called a 'sport' by your old mates, then forget other considerations, renounce them, walk away and have nothing more to do with that crowd. [9] If you don't like that, then commit to the opposite course with all your heart. Join the louche set, become one of the degenerates – do as they do and indulge your every impulse and desire. Jump around and yell at a musical performance, what's to stop you now?

[10] Such different roles don't mix. You can't play the part of both Thersites and Agamemnon. If you want to be Thersites, you should be bald and crippled. Agamemnon needs to be tall and handsome, and a leader with a genuine love for the people under his command.

15

To those intent on living quietly

[1] Remember, it isn't just desire for power and money that makes a man humble and deferential towards others, but also desire for the opposite – for a life of peace and quiet, of travel and scholarship. It is a general rule that externals of any kind, if we attach importance to them, make us subject to somebody. [2] It makes no difference whether we wish to be a senator, or wish *not* to be one; whether we desire to have office, or to avoid it; whether we say, 'I can't do anything, unfortunately, I'm tied to my books like a stiff,' or, 'Sadly, I have no leisure for study.' [3] A book is an external, just like office or public honours. [4] Why do you want to read anyway – for the sake of amusement or mere erudition? Those are poor, fatuous pretexts. Reading should serve the goal of attaining peace; if it doesn't make you peaceful, what good is it?

[5] 'But it does help with that – which is exactly why I regret being deprived of it.'

What kind of peace is this that is so easily shattered – not by the emperor or even by a friend of the emperor, but by a crow, a street musician, a cold, or a thousand other annoyances? True peace is characterized by nothing so much as steadiness and imperturbability.

[6] Now I am being called upon for some purpose. I answer the call determined to observe the right limits;

to act with restraint, but also with confidence, devoid of desire or aversion towards externals. [7] At the same time I observe other people's words and actions – not maliciously, in order to judge or ridicule them, but to better assess whether I engage in any of the same behaviour. 'How should I stop, then?' 'Once I was liable to the same mistakes, but, thanks to God, no longer . . .'

[8] Well, isn't it just as worthwhile to have devoted and applied yourself to this goal as to have read or written fifty pages? After all, when you are eating, you don't wish you were reading, you are content to be eating in a manner consistent with the principles you learned from your reading; likewise when you bathe or exercise. [9] So be consistent in other respects – when you meet Caesar, or when you meet some random passer-by. If you keep yourself calm, poised and dignified, [10] if you observe rather than are observed, if you don't envy people with greater success, don't let externals disconcert you – if you do all this, what more do you need? [11] Books? Yes, but how, or for what purpose?

'Isn't reading a kind of preparation for life?'

But life is composed of things other than books. It is as if an athlete, on entering the stadium, were to complain that he's not outside exercising. [12] This was the goal of your exercise, of your weights, your practice ring and your training partners. You want them now that the time to exploit them has arrived? [13] Or it's as if, in the matter of assent, when faced with impressions, instead of distinguishing which ones are convincing and which are not, we prefer to read a book entitled *On Comprehensive Impressions*.

[14] So what accounts for such behaviour? The fact that our reading and our writing have never aimed at using in conformity with nature the impressions that we encounter in real life. Instead, it is enough for us to learn what is written on the topic and be able to explicate it before someone else; it is enough if we can analyse an argument or develop a hypothesis.

[15] Consequently, there is bound to be frustration when you exert yourself. You desire what is not in your control: fine, but be prepared to be refused, to be frustrated, to come up empty-handed. [16] If, on the other hand, we read books entitled *On Impulse* not just out of idle curiosity, but in order to exercise impulse correctly; books entitled *On Desire* and *On Aversion* so as not to fail to get what we desire or fall victim to what we would rather avoid; and books entitled *On Moral Obligation* in order to honour our relationships and never do anything that clashes or conflicts with this principle; [17] then we wouldn't get frustrated and grow impatient with our reading. Instead we would be satisfied to act accordingly. And rather than reckon, as we are used to doing, [18] 'How many lines I read, or wrote, today,' we would pass in review how 'I applied impulse today the way the philosophers recommend, how I desisted from desire, and practised aversion only on matters that are under my control. I wasn't flustered by *A* or angered by *B*; I was patient, restrained and cooperative.' That way we will be able to thank God for things that we truly should be grateful for.

[19] As it is, though, we fail to realize how little we differ from the mass of men, the only difference being that

they are afraid they will not hold office, while you are afraid you will. Don't act that way; [20] if you must laugh at someone who is anxious that he won't hold office, then laugh at yourself as well. Someone suffering from rabies and afraid of water is no better off than someone suffering from fever and ready to drain the ocean dry. [21] If you would dictate to circumstance, how can you emulate Socrates, who said, 'If it pleases the gods, so be it'?

Do you think Socrates would have been as ready to serve on so many campaigns if he had longed to linger in the Academy or the Lyceum every day, conversing with young men? No, he would have groused and grumbled, 'Hell, here I am in misery when I might be back in the Lyceum sunning myself.' Is that your job, sunning yourself? [22] Isn't it rather to be happy, unflappable and equal to every occasion? How could he have remained Socrates, had he yielded to disaffection? How would he have been the same man who wrote hymns of praise behind prison walls?

[23] Just keep in mind: the more we value things outside our control, the less control we have. And among things outside our control is not only access to, but relief from, public office; not just work, but leisure too.

[24] 'So now I have to live my life among the mob?'

The mob? You mean crowds? What's wrong with crowds? Imagine you're at Olympia, in the middle of the festival, where you will likewise find some people shouting while others conduct business on the side, and everywhere people are jostling one another. The baths, too, are a madhouse. Yet which of us does not enjoy the party, and regret when it's time to leave? [25] Don't grow peevish about trivialities. 'The vinegar is bad, it's sharp; the honey's bad, it upsets my constitution; I didn't like the vegetables.'

[26] Similarly, someone says, 'I don't like leisure, it's boring; I don't like crowds, they're a nuisance.' But if events ordain that you spend time either alone or with just a few other people, look upon it as tranquillity and play along with it for the duration. Talk to yourself, train your thoughts and shape your preconceptions. If, on the contrary, you happen upon a crowd, call it a sporting event, a festival or celebration, [27] and try to keep holiday with the people. What could better please a person who loves his fellow man than the sight of them in numbers? We like to see herds of cows or horses, we delight in the sight of a fleet of boats; why hate the sight of a gathering of human beings?

[28] 'But they deafen me with their shouting.'

So your hearing is offended; what does it have to do with you? Your power of using impressions isn't diminished, is it? Who can keep you from using desire and aversion, or choice and refusal, in conformity with nature? No mob is big enough for that.

[29] Just keep in mind the central questions: 'What is mine, what is not mine? What has been given to me? What does God want me to do, or not do, now?' [30] It wasn't long ago he wanted you to take time off, to commune with yourself, to read, write and attend classes on these subjects – all by way of preparation, because you had the time available. Now, however, he's saying to you, 'It's high time you were tested. Show us what you've learned, show us how well you've trained. How long do

you plan on working out alone? We want to know whether you are champion material or a touring professional push-over. [31] So don't make difficulties, no public match is devoid of commotion. There have to be trainers, support-ers, many judges and many people in the stands.'

[32] 'But I was hoping to lead a peaceful life.'

Well, then, mope and be miserable, as you should be. What greater punishment do you deserve for ignoring and defying God's will than to be sad, disgruntled and malcontent – unhappy, in short, and ill-fated? Don't you want to be free of all that?

[33] 'But how can I do it?'

You've often heard how – you need to suspend desire completely, and train aversion only on things within your power. You should dissociate yourself from everything outside yourself – the body, possessions, reputation, books, applause, as well as office or lack of office. Because a pref-erence for any of them immediately makes you a slave, a subordinate, and prone to disappointment. [34] Keep Cleanthes' verse handy:

Lead me, Zeus, lead me, Destiny.

Do I have to go to Rome? Then I go to Rome. To Gyara? All right, I go to Gyara instead. To Athens? Then Athens it is. To jail? Well then I go to jail. [35] But if you ever think, 'When do we get to go to Athens?' you are already lost. Either you're going to be depressed when your wish is not realized or foolishly pleased with your-self if it is, overjoyed for the wrong reasons. And next time, if you're not so lucky, you'll grow disconsolate when events are not so much to your liking. [36] Give them all up.

'But Athens is lovely.'

It would be lovelier still if you could secure happiness, free of emotion, poised and dependent on no one except yourself.

'And Rome is all crowds and sycophancy.'

[37] But the reward for enduring such inconveniences is peace. So if this is the time for them, why not conquer your aversion? Why endure them like a donkey hit by sticks? [38] Otherwise, look, you will always have to serve the person who is able to secure your release, or the person who can block your way. You will have to serve him the way you would an evil deity.

[39] There is one road to peace and happiness (keep the thought nearby morning, noon and night): renunciation of externals; regarding nothing as your own; handing over everything to fortune and the deity. Leave those things in the care of the same people God appointed to govern them, [40] while you devote yourself to the one thing that is truly yours and that no one can obstruct; make *that* the focus of all your reading, your writing and your lecture attendance.

[41] I cannot call somebody 'hard-working' knowing only that they read and write. Even if 'all night long' is added, I cannot say it – not until I know the focus of all this energy. You don't call someone 'hard-working' who stays up nights with their girlfriend. No more do I. [42] If the goal is glory, I call them ambitious; if it's money, I call them avaricious. [43] If, however, their efforts aim at improving the mind, then – and only then – do I call them hard-working. [44] Never praise or blame people on common grounds; look to their judgements exclusively. Because

that is the determining factor, which makes everyone's actions either good or bad.

[45] Bearing all this in mind, welcome present circumstances and accept the things whose time has arrived. [46] Be happy when you find that doctrines you have learned and analysed are being tested by real events. If you've succeeded in removing or reducing the tendency to be mean and critical, or thoughtless, or foul-mouthed, or careless, or nonchalant; if old interests no longer engage you, at least not to the same extent; then every day can be a feast day – today because you acquitted yourself well in one set of circumstances, tomorrow because of another.

[47] How much better cause is this to celebrate than becoming consul or governor; because you have yourself to thank, and the gods. Remember, then, who is responsible for the gift, to whom it was given, and for what reason. [48] With these thoughts, can you doubt where your future happiness lies, or how you will best please God? Is it not the same distance to God everywhere? Are not events equally visible from every vantage point?

THE STORY OF PENGUIN CLASSICS

Before 1946 ... 'Classics' are mainly the domain of academics and students; readable editions for everyone else are almost unheard of. This all changes when a little-known classicist, E. V. Rieu, presents Penguin founder Allen Lane with the translation of Homer's *Odyssey* that he has been working on in his spare time.

1946 Penguin Classics debuts with *The Odyssey*, which promptly sells three million copies. Suddenly, classics are no longer for the privileged few.

1950s Rieu, now series editor, turns to professional writers for the best modern, readable translations, including Dorothy L. Sayers's *Inferno* and Robert Graves's unexpurgated *Twelve Caesars*.

1960s The Classics are given the distinctive black covers that have remained a constant throughout the life of the series. Rieu retires in 1964, hailing the Penguin Classics list as 'the greatest educative force of the twentieth century.'

1970s A new generation of translators swells the Penguin Classics ranks, introducing readers of English to classics of world literature from more than twenty languages. The list grows to encompass more history, philosophy, science, religion and politics.

1980s The Penguin American Library launches with titles such as *Uncle Tom's Cabin*, and joins forces with Penguin Classics to provide the most comprehensive library of world literature available from any paperback publisher.

1990s The launch of Penguin Audiobooks brings the classics to a listening audience for the first time, and in 1999 the worldwide launch of the Penguin Classics website extends their reach to the global online community.

The 21st Century Penguin Classics are completely redesigned for the first time in nearly twenty years. This world-famous series now consists of more than 1300 titles, making the widest range of the best books ever written available to millions – and constantly redefining what makes a 'classic'.

The Odyssey continues ...

The best books ever written

PENGUIN CLASSICS

SINCE 1946

Find out more at www.penguinclassics.com

Throughout history, some books have changed the world. They have transformed the way we see ourselves – and each other. They have inspired debate, dissent, war and revolution. They have enlightened, outraged, provoked and comforted. They have enriched lives – and destroyed them. Now PENGUIN brings you the works of the great thinkers, pioneers, radicals and visionaries whose ideas shook civilization and helped make us who we are.

In this personal and practical guide to moral self-improvement and living a good life, the second-century philosopher Epictetus tackles questions of freedom and imprisonment, stubbornness and fear, family, friendship and love, and leaves an intriguing document of daily life in the classical world.

read more

ISBN 978-0-141-19235-2

9 780141 192352

penguinclassics.com

U.K. £7.99
CAN. $16.99
Cover artwork:
David Pearson

ALBERT CAMUS

—

Reflections on the Guillotine